IMPROVE YOUR MEMORY

IMPROVE YOUR
MEMORY

**LEARN FASTER, RETAIN MORE AND
UNLOCK YOUR BRAIN'S POTENTIAL**

PETER HOLLINS

Published by
Rupa Publications India Pvt. Ltd 2023
7/16, Ansari Road, Daryaganj
New Delhi 110002

Sales Centres:
Allahabad Bengaluru Chennai
Hyderabad Jaipur Kathmandu
Kolkata Mumbai

Copyright © PKCS Media Inc. 2023
Published under arrangement with PKCS Media,
Inc. through TLL Literary Agency

The views and opinions expressed in this book are the author's own
and the facts are as reported by him which have been verified to the extent
possible, and the publishers are not in any way liable for the same.

All rights reserved.
No part of this publication may be reproduced, transmitted,
or stored in a retrieval system, in any form or by any means,
electronic, mechanical, photocopying, recording or otherwise,
without the prior permission of the publisher.

P-ISBN: 978-93-5520-992-4
E-ISBN: 978-93-5520-993-1

First impression 2023

10 9 8 7 6 5 4 3 2 1

The moral right of the author has been asserted.

Printed in India

This book is sold subject to the condition that it shall not, by way of
trade or otherwise, be lent, resold, hired out, or otherwise circulated,
without the publisher's prior consent, in any form of binding or
cover other than that in which it is published.

CONTENTS

Introduction   7

1. How Memory Works   10
2. All About Forgetting   19
3. The Roles of Stress, Sleep, and Exercise   29
4. Memory Improvement Methods Pt. I   38
5. Memory Improvement Methods Pt. II   49
6. Memory Improvement Methods Pt. III   60
7. The Memory Palace Technique   71
8. Developing Photographic Memory   79
9. Phenomena of Memory   87
10. Boost Your Brain   98

Conclusion   108
Summary Guide   110

INTRODUCTION

I was 10 years old, and my entire class was tasked with memorizing all 50 state capitals.

It seemed like an utterly impossible task. I was in fifth grade, and I had just gotten my first bike. I still used training wheels. How was I supposed to be able to recall, without looking at a map, all 50 state capitals and the states they were in? Amazingly, this was a task that every single child in my class passed, but I'll get to that in a second.

Memory is a fascinating concept for most people. It's clear that our minds can work like steel traps one day, yet an Etch A Sketch that gets erased almost immediately other days. What happens inside our heads when either one of those happens?

Improve Your Memory is a book that sheds light onto exactly how memory works, what it likes, and how to take advantage of it. Our memories are fickle, but attracted to very specific things like moths to a flame.

At the beginning of the school year, my fifth grade teacher started playing a song in the background while he wasn't actively teaching or lecturing. At first, we didn't pay attention. But by the middle of the school year, most of us were able to sing along with most of the song's lyrics.

Guess what the lyrics were saying?

The song was written and performed by a set of teachers with some appropriately punny name, and the song was designed specifically to teach children the 50 state capitals of the United States. The capitals were set to a catchy guitar tune with a funny story about a German couple touring the country and all of the odd things they saw, like a camel in Harrisburg, Pennsylvania, and a man eating his own shoe in Helena, Montana. My teacher had been playing this in the background for months, and we had learned it without even realizing it.

He had *Miyagi'd* us!

This is a process from the movie *The Karate Kid*, where a martial arts master teaches his student essential defenses and attacks through making him paint fences and labor through other household chores. It was learning while unaware, which is probably the best way to teach children. Now that I've done a significant amount of psychological and neurological research on human performance, I instantly realized how genius the state capital song was when I remembered it.

First, the song itself was a mnemonic—a device for giving meaning to a set of information as a way of more easily memorizing it. The most common mnemonics you will have heard of are acronyms or acrostics, but a song and the associated rhymes that were in the song made it so that if you hummed the melody, you would probably be able to recite the lyrics as well.

Second, the song incorporated flashy, weird, and outlandish

Introduction

visuals. The writers of the song realized that human memory prefers that which stands out, as opposed to that which blends in. It wouldn't be memorable to say that a man had breakfast in Helena, Montana. Instead, they used a man eating his own shoe as an odd action that would make kids sit up and take notice. The fact that I still remember a few of those lyrics to this day attests to how effective those jarring visuals were.

I didn't effectively utilize any similar memory tactics through school, but I sure wish I would have consciously discovered the techniques that are described in this book—I would have gotten better grades. I could have made my life easier, and all the while, doing so unconsciously.

But memory improvement doesn't stop at school. Any time you want to remember a grocery list, or even remember someone's name, it's a test for our memory. It's a skill that enables learning, reading, and even speaking better in life. It underlies everything we want to achieve. Will your memory pass the test?

To your success,

Pete

1
HOW MEMORY WORKS

When we think of the concept of memory, there are a few things that spring into mind. First, we might think of the amnesiac we see in movies—unable to remember anything from the point of an accident, and forever stuck in the past. We also might think about how talented and intelligent elephants are as a result of their memories. Finally, you might think back to your school days when you were desperately trying to cram knowledge into your head for a test you hadn't studied for at all.

Memory is all of these things and more. Our world is created and perceived entirely through our memories, and they are unique to anyone else's. There are spectacular disorders like amnesia, and methods of cramming knowledge into your head, that can actually affect your long-term memory.

Memory is such a broad topic, and there are so many ways to tackle it, but let's start with the basics. What is memory, and how does it work?

The easiest way of defining memory is this: memory is our ability to process the external world and turn our experiences into information that is filed away for later use. Whether we want to memorize a recipe or phone number, they are stored in our brains by the same process and recalled by the same process. Memory allows us to learn from previous experiences and prevent us from making the same mistakes, and it also records our daily lives for analysis and examination. It can be argued that we are but the sum of our memories, and that memories comprise the world we live in.

After the present moment passes, all that remains is a memory of it, and the memory can be strong or weak depending on a variety of factors we'll cover later in this book.

On the physiological and biological level, memory is but activity between specific neurons in the brain. There are the neurons which process external stimuli and then pass electrical signals to neurons that deal with working memory, then long-term memory, if we are lucky (or supremely unlucky). It sounds like an organized system, but in reality, memory is more akin to an ancient library—the shelves are overstuffed, books often disappear, and there are a dozen hallways leading to parts unknown. Generally, you are able to find what you want, but sometimes you will be completely lost, and other times it takes an errant smell or distant reminder to conjure up the memory you were seeking. Along the way, you might stumble upon a book that makes you cry or laugh, and it will be at the back of your mind for years to come.

Memory, of course, is heavily related to learning. If memory is a storage system that exists within specific neural pathways, then learning is about changing neural pathways to adapt one's behavior and thinking to the emergence of new information. They depend on each other because the goal of learning is to assimilate new knowledge into memory, and memory is useless without the ability to learn more.

Memory is how we store and retrieve information for use, and there are three steps to creating a memory. An error in any of these steps will result in knowledge that is not effectively converted to memory—a weak memory, or the feeling of, "I can't remember his name, but he was wearing purple …"

1. Encoding
2. Storage
3. Retrieval

Encoding is the step of processing information through your senses. We do this constantly, and you are doing it right now. We encode information both consciously and subconsciously through all of our senses. If you are reading a book, you are using your eyes to encode information, but how much attention and focus are you actually using? The more attention and focus to devote to an activity, the more conscious your encoding becomes—otherwise, it can be said that you subconsciously encode information, like listening to music at a café or seeing traffic pass you by at a red traffic light.

How much focus and attention you devote also determines how strong the memory is, and consequently, whether that memory only makes it to your short-term memory, or if it passes through the gate to your long-term memory.

Storage is the next step after you've experienced information

How Memory Works

with your senses and encoded it. What happens to the information once it passes through your eyes or ears? There are three choices for where this information can go, and they determine whether it's a memory that you will consciously know exists. There are essentially three memory systems: sensory memory, short-term memory, and long-term memory.

Sensory memory is the first level of memory, and it stores information for only an instant. This is literally just information about the senses, such as the way the chair feels, the wind from a car that passes you by, or the music playing in the background of an elevator. Sensory memory is the biggest net in the sense that it catches just about everything about your current experience, but most of it disintegrates immediately because it is not deemed important. The way a chair feels against your arm is not integral to your experience at that moment, so it is only registered briefly within your sensory memory, then discarded. Hearing the music is not important, so it vanishes quickly as well. However, listening to a professor speak about your favorite subject is deemed to have significance, so it will certainly make it past this stage of memory.

Just think of sensory memory as a buffer for the rest of your brain. It takes everything in and filters it effectively. Of course, our brains aren't perfect, and that's why we forget or overlook things. We process most of our sensory memories on a subconscious level, which is what you would expect for something that will be processed in under 500 milliseconds.

Information makes it past sensory memory and into short-term memory with attention and focus. The chair underneath you might be processed subconsciously, but if you consciously felt the chair and thought to yourself that it felt like sandpaper, there is a decent chance you will remember that sentiment at the end of the day.

A small portion of information is then transferred from sensory memory to short-term memory. It's impossible for everything to transfer because it would mean you remember *everything* about *everything*—while this may sound convenient, it would be an overload for your brain and it is impossible to achieve. People who have exceptional memories have been found to suffer impairment in planning, focus, and attention tasks. Your brain is doing you a favor by filtering here.

Short-term memory is what we're most familiar with, and it can retain information for roughly 20 seconds on average. For example, if you are looking up a phone number, you will likely be able to remember most of it without rehearsing it too heavily for 20 seconds. But beyond that, it's likely vanished from your mind and you will have to look it up again.

Think of your short-term memory as an Etch A Sketch pad that is shaken and erased every 20 seconds. It can hold and remember some information, but not that much, and not for that long. If you have a list of groceries you want to buy, short-term memory isn't going to work for you because it will take you some time to get to the store and walk around—by the time you get there, the information will probably have left your brain.

On the other hand, if you have a list of fifteen items and you are already at the store, this also won't work because it's simply too much information – it's beyond the capacity of short-term memory. Short-term memory is simply temporary, in most cases, and is designed that way for the same reason that sensory memory is. It helps your brain filter what is important and what is not.

Imagine if you could only fixate on the feeling of the chair, and as a result, you didn't remember anything from a lecture you attended. Clearly, some things are more important than the others, and the brain has a good baseline for that.

Information will vanish from your short-term memory unless you rehearse it, such as saying a phone number out loud, or giving it some type of meaning or significance. We might remember the phone number of our first significant other because it was so important to us as a teenager, which is an example of a memory forming from emotional significance and motivation. That would certainly make the leap into long-term memory, but most phone numbers would not.

Long-term memory is where a photo is taken of that Post-It. It is where memories become a real, physical manifestation as a result of neurons making connections. Long-term memory can be split into two main categories: explicit and implicit.

Explicit memories are facts and information, such as the capital of Romania (Bucharest) or the colors of the rainbow (ROY G BIV). We have tried to remember these facts and experiences for later use. There are two kinds of explicit memory: episodic and semantic. Episodic memory is memory of experiences and events that happened to you, while semantic memory is more about facts and general knowledge. Going sailing is an episodic memory, while knowing the parts of the boat are semantic memory. This is also called declarative memory.

Implicit memories are habits, skills, and even muscle memory, like riding a bike, signing your signature, or brushing your teeth. These are all subconscious and not processed with intent. They are just imprints in your memory that your experiences leave. It can even be something as simple as knowing your way around your own house, or where your shower is located. This is also called procedural memory—things you can pick up and do or recall after long periods of time as "second nature."

The last step of the memory process is retrieval, which is essentially when you remember something. You might be able to recall it from nothing, or you might need a cue to bring the memory up. Other memories might only be memorized in a sequence or as part of a whole, like reciting the ABCs and then realizing you need to sing it to remember how it goes. Usually, however much attention you devoted to the storage and encoding phases of memory determines just how easy it is to retrieve those memories. Most of memory isn't necessarily focused on retrieval—it's focused on the storage aspect, and what you can do to force memories from sensory and short-term areas into long-term areas.

Think about when you cram for a test. You want information you experience to be in your brain for perhaps 24 hours, which means it has to exist beyond short-term memory, and certainly beyond sensory memory. You might not care if you remember this information about the French Revolution at the end of the year, so you will reach a level of attention and focus that will push the information into the hazy area between short-term and long-term memory. In reality, what's happening is that you will rehearse the information enough to make a very faint imprint on your long-term memory.

So to recap and provide some structure, here is what the memory process looks like:

- Encoding
- Storage
  - Sensory Memory
  - Short-Term Memory
  - Long-Term Memory
    - Explicit and Declarative Memory
    - Implicit and Procedural Memory
    - Episodic Memory
    - Semantic Memory
- Retrieval

Here's a quick example to illustrate how some of these aspects all work together.

Suppose I walk into a café and order a cappuccino. It's what I usually order, so nothing notable has happened, and nothing will probably make it past my sensory memory at this point besides the fact that I consciously went into the café. However, suppose I look across the café and suddenly see famous actor Morgan Freeman. This is something that will immediately grab my attention and focus, so it will definitely go into my short-term memory, and probably my long-term memory because it is so notable. This is an example of explicit, declarative, and episodic memory because it is an experience I am remembering and also a fact.

Just when you thought you had a clear understanding, I want to briefly dive into the biology and neurology of memory. Just kidding.

This isn't a textbook, and I know it's more important for you to learn ways to store memories more effectively. For our purposes, it is enough to understand that there are literal physical changes to brain structure (mostly in the prefrontal cortex) when memories are pushed into long-term memory. Most of us function primarily within the limited Post-It of our short-term memory, and this book is aimed at pushing the information you deem important into your long-term memory.

Instead of your brain deciding what's important, you can begin to decide for yourself and remember exactly what you want, be it a phone number, equations for a math test, or the directions to your mother's home.

2
ALL ABOUT FORGETTING

When we talk about memory, the first issue many people want to address is forgetting. We don't actually want to improve our memory; we just want to get better at not forgetting.

Why do we forget? Why can't we remember this fact? How did we ever let something slip from our brains?

As you now know, it's not as simple as forgetting—forgetting is usually a failure or shortcoming in the storage process. Think of it this way: the problem isn't that you can't find the information in your brain; it's that the information wasn't embedded strongly enough in your brain to begin with. Unfortunately, that's not how most people conceive of forgetting, and it subsequently causes them to approach better memory in interesting, but flawed ways.

Sometimes it is easier to think about forgetting as a failure in learning. There are generally three different ways you retrieve, or access your memories:

1. Recall
2. Recognition
3. Relearning

Recall is when you remember a memory without external cues. It's when you can recite something on command in a vacuum. For example, looking at a blank piece of paper and then writing down the capitals of all of the countries of the world. When you can recall something, you have the strongest memory of it. You have either rehearsed it enough or attached enough significance to it so that it is an incredibly strong memory within your long-term memory. Of course, because recall represents the strongest level of memory, it's also typically the toughest to achieve. It would typically require hours of rehearsal or study to get anywhere close to this. When we study, we want information to enter this realm, but we will usually settle for the next type of memory retrieval.

Recognition is when you can conjure up your memory in the presence of an external cue. It's when you might not be able to remember something by pure recall, but if you get a small clue or reminder, you will be able to remember it. For example, you might not be able to remember all of the capitals of the world, but if you got a clue such as the first letter of the capital, or something that rhymes with the capital, it would be fairly easy to state it. When we cram information, this is typically what we end up with. This is also how mnemonics and similar memory devices work. We know we aren't able to definitively store and recall so many pieces of information with a massive amount of rehearsal, so we work on chunking information into easily recognizable cues.

Relearning is undoubtedly the weakest form of recall. It occurs when you are relearning or reviewing information and it takes you less effort each subsequent time. For example, if you read a list of country capitals on Monday and it takes you 30 minutes, it should take you 15 minutes the next day, and so on. Unfortunately, this is where we mostly lie on a daily basis. We might be familiar with a concept, but we haven't committed enough of it to memory to avoid essentially relearning it when we look at it again. This is what happens when we are new to a topic, or we've forgotten most of it already. When you're in the relearning stage, you essentially haven't taken anything past the barrier of short-term memory into long-term memory.

Everyone forgets, and this chapter investigates why. Often, it is related to an error or shortcoming in storage or recall, as you just read. Forgetting is actually a blanket term for many errors related to memory, such as *memory decay, failure to retrieve, poor encoding, motivated forgetting, retrieval interference,* and *brain injury.*

Memory Decay

Memory decay is the simple, yet sad fact that memories, even long-term ones, will fade with time. Something you might have known like the back of your hand when you were a teenager will likely be lost when you turn 30, unless you tend to revisit or rehearse it. Our brains are constantly prioritizing new information, and it is thought that the brain essentially has only a limited amount of space for conscious memories. Therefore, memories tend to decay and fade over time from long-term memory, and of course, they decay every day from sensory and short-term memory. Time isn't the only factor that leads to decay, as people can sometimes remember things from their teenage years more readily than what they had for lunch that same day. It also depends on storage, encoding, and significance, but memory does have the tendency to decay over time.

If you haven't accessed a memory in years, the brain literally sees no use for it, and you forget it.

Typically, the rate at which memory decays follows a very specific pattern known as the forgetting curve, discovered and studied by Hermann Ebbinghaus.

Failure to Retrieve

This manner of forgetting is when there is a failure to retrieve because there is an absence of clues or hints. Earlier, I mentioned that most of memory relies on cues and contextual significance. If you are put into an empty room and expect to remember the name of your soccer coach when you were young, that might be difficult, but the name might spring into your brain instantly when you run on grass. The failure to retrieve means that memories are frequently tied into our environment, people, or even sensory experiences, and memory is rarely stored as a fact by itself. This is why, as you'll read later, it's often helpful to involve all five of your senses when attempting to commit something to memory. If the fact you are trying to remember is one sign for your memory to find, then using all five senses creates five signs for your memory to find.

When we are devoid of cues, we forget, and when we are devoid of cues for long enough, we may just forget the information permanently.

Poor Encoding

Recall that encoding is when you experience information or stimulation. An example of poor encoding would be reading while you are simultaneously watching television, or listening to a lecture while shopping on your laptop.

You aren't really paying attention enough for your brain to encode the information. Essentially, it means the information hasn't quite entered your brain because your attention was split, or just not focused on the information itself. If information is not encoded properly, there's no way it can be stored very well, which of course leads to very quick forgetting.

You can also think of this as simple absentmindedness. You failed to pay attention, so there is nothing encoded for you to remember or recall.

If you are meeting a friend and listening to their story about their weekend skiing, and you are fumbling with your phone and returning texts at the same time, you aren't going to remember your friend's story very well. This is an input problem—like the receiver in a radio being too weak to form an intelligible message. You forget because it was never really in your mind to start with.

Motivated Forgetting

Some people might want to overlook this aspect of forgetting, but it is worth a mention, at the very least. This term comes from the infamous psychologist Sigmund Freud, who is best known for his theories on being attracted to our own parents and our lives being run entirely by our subconscious desires.

Motivated forgetting is essentially the concept of memory repression. It's when the subconscious acts to protect itself from traumatic events and pushes unpleasant memories into the dark recesses of the mind. If there was a history of trauma with a parent as a child, for example, someone might engage in motivated forgetting to allow them to function better on a daily basis as opposed to reacting to authority figures and caregivers hostilely and without trust.

Motivated forgetting is a defense mechanism that isn't truly forgetting—it's building a mental wall around something that is unpleasant to think about.

Of course, sometimes the opposite of this happens, where we are unable to stop fixating on something that is disturbing to us. For example, the stress and anxiety of a big test can keep us awake until 4 AM.

Retrieval Interference

According to retrieval interference, people forget because of interference from other learned information. Memory is a fierce battleground where things are purged every day in favor of something else significant or rehearsed, whether intentional or not. It only makes sense that there are a limited amount of things you can recall or recite at any given moment. There's too much information, or there is similar information such that you get confused and mix them together.

Essentially, you forget because something else has taken precedence or priority over the information you want.

The more dangerous possibility of retrieval interference is when you mistakenly retrieve a memory of a dream or fantasy you had in place of reality—for example, if you vividly imagined that you slapped someone across the face and then apologized to them later in real life. This is the misattribution of a fantasy to a real memory, and is far more common than we might realize. In fact, it's the reason that eyewitness testimonies are generally seen as unreliable in legal settings.

We can easily dream experiences and get them mixed up with real memories, and we can also be easily influenced by others—for example, if someone was to badger you and continually ask you if you remember the time that you went skiing together. Eventually, it would cause you to question your own memory, and you might even acquiesce and agree that you went skiing together at some point.

Physical Injury

We'll go over this in more detail later, but physical injury to the brain can cause multiple types of amnesia. Briefly, anterograde amnesia is the lack of ability to remember events after the injury, while retrograde amnesia is the lack of ability to remember events before an injury. If Jack is struck in the head and can't remember his name, he has retrograde amnesia. If he cannot remember where he is located (the hospital), he has anterograde amnesia.

Biased Memories

This is when there are memories present, and perhaps even committed to long-term memory, but they become skewed as a result of our internal biases. This causes the memory to become wrong and not represent reality, but rather, how we view an event or concept as filtered through our perspective.

We remember our pasts as a reflection of our values and beliefs. This, unfortunately, gives us the ability to rewrite our memories, often unconsciously, according to those values and beliefs; for example, we might want to remember that we were great soccer players when we were young, despite the reality that we were terrible. This belief would cause us to remember only the positive plays we made, and forget all the times when we tripped over our own feet and scored goals for the other team. The memory is there, but it is inaccurate because of our biases. Only certain parts are forgotten, which is often more dangerous than entire memories being gone.

All About Forgetting

The Forgetting Curve

The forgetting curve is a concept pioneered by Hermann Ebbinghaus. Below is a picture of the forgetting curve, courtesy of wranx.com.

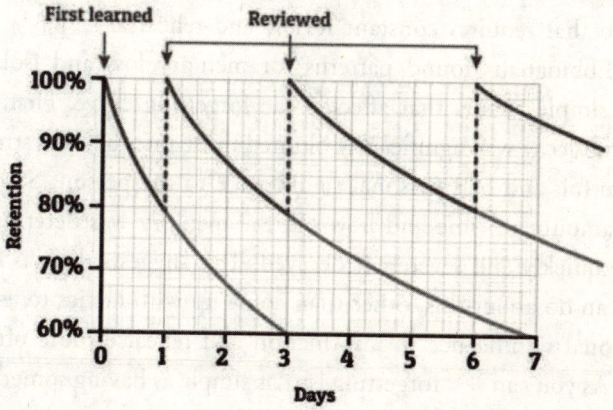

This shows the rate of memory decay and forgetting over time, if there is no attempt to move this information into long-term memory. If you read something about the French Revolution on Monday, then it's typically expected that you will remember only half of it after four days, and retain as little as 30% at around a week's time. If you don't review what you've learned, it's very likely you will only retain 10% of what you learned about the French Revolution. However, if you review and rehearse it, you can see in the graph above how you will retain and memorize more over time. You will bump the retention level back up to 100%, and then the graph will start to become shallower, indicating less decay.

The goal with the knowledge of the forgetting curve is to make the curve shallower; to make it resemble a horizontal line as much as possible. That would indicate very little decay, and to do that requires constant review and rehearsal.

Ebbinghaus found patterns for memory loss and isolated two simple factors that affected the forgetting curve. First, the rate of decay was significantly blunted if the memory was strong, powerful, and had personal significance to the person. Second, the amount of time and how old the memory was determined how quickly and severely it decayed. This suggests there is little we can do about this, other than come up with tactics to assign personal significance to information and rehearse more often.

As you can see, forgetting isn't as simple as having something on the tip of your tongue or rummaging through the stores of your brain. There are very specific processes that make it a near-miracle that we actually retain as much as we do.

Being able to recall information is always the goal, but more realistically, we should be shooting for recognition and to learn how to expertly use cues and hints in our daily lives. I may not be able to recite the lyrics of my favorite songs, but I can sure remember them if I hear the melody.

3

THE ROLES OF STRESS, SLEEP, AND EXERCISE

If you think the title of this chapter sounds like it belongs in a health and wellness book, you'd be right. It highlights the importance of one's overall physical and mental health on our brain's ability to memorize and create memories.

After all, the brain, for all its manifestations and conceptions, is a physical piece of flesh and blood that gets tired, needs fuel, and doesn't always function at its best. The brain, just like any other piece of physical flesh and blood, has optimal conditions under which it functions and creates memories.

The brain consumes glucose and is composed mostly of water. It needs time to recover and has its own limits. When you think about it, it should be obvious that overall bodily health should and will affect your memory's abilities.

If there is a runner and she has a race tomorrow, do you think stress, sleep, and exercise will play a role in getting her ready for the race? She will have regularly exercised to be in her best shape possible, she would reduce her stress and focus on what she needs to, and sleep as much as possible that night so she is fresh as possible.

Now, take the brain.

Will you retain information better after getting only three hours of sleep, or when you have a full eight hours? What about if you had to work 90 hours one week, versus 35 another? Finally, what if you had a long debate with a friend—are you going to feel fresh and ready to consume information?

Just like an athlete, the memory must be ready for performance, and the factors of stress, sleep, and exercise greatly influence that. Let's begin our mini tour of how neurological health is directly correlated to improving your memory.

Stress

Stress is one of the biggest influences on the brain's health. If you want a clear and concrete illustration, you don't have to look any further than any veteran or trauma victim suffering from post-traumatic stress disorder (PTSD) and how their lives are negatively affected. They literally lack the ability to function in daily life because they are so tense, and they are likely to snap at any given moment as an outlet for their anxiety and fear.

A plethora of research has found that both chronic and acute stress impact the brain's health and memory systems in hugely negative ways. This is in large part due to the body's physiological response to stress. But first, it will be helpful to define the difference between the two main types of stress:

chronic stress and acute stress.

Chronic stress is simply when you are under ongoing stress for a relatively long period of time—something as small as being under a constant heavy load at work, or dealing with a relationship that is frequently combative. These are the small sources of stresses that seem insignificant until you look at the cumulative effects. When we are experiencing chronic stress (again, the amount of highly variable and relative to the person's tolerance), our body is in a state of physiological arousal. This is known as the fight-or-flight response, and it's our body's main defense mechanism when it senses stress or fear.

It was once useful millennia ago when the terms "fight" and "flight" were truly taken literally—if the body sensed a stressor or reason to be in fear, it would put itself on the highest levels of alertness and be prepared for a fight to the death if necessary, or running away as quickly as possible. In either case, the body's hormones, heart rate, and blood pressure are highly elevated. The main stress hormone, cortisol, is released in spades and has been implicated in causing the alertness.

So if you are under chronic stress, you are permanently in this fight-or-flight mode of alertness and spades of cortisol. Your body will very rarely reach the relaxation phase, which is known as a state of homeostasis. In other words, chronic stress makes you alert and physiologically aroused *all the time*. This is exhausting both physically and mentally, and has the effect of shrinking your brain. Studies have shown that chronic stress has caused as big as a 14% decrease in hippocampal volume, which is startling.

The hippocampus is one of the main areas for memory processing and storage in the brain. Another study (Pasquali, 2006) showed that memory in rats was negatively affected when the rats were exposed to cats, which presumably caused stress. The rats that were exposed to cats far more routinely were unable to locate certain entrances and exits. It was both cute and fascinating.

Chronic stress will cause all of those negative effects in you, and the difficult part is you may not realize you are under chronic stress because it has become normalized for you. It is just like when your shoulders tense up—you probably don't realize it until someone points it out and you can see the contrast between being relaxed and being tensed up.

The cumulative effects of being constantly on edge, paranoid, unable to focus, and feeling despair and overwhelmed will catch up to you. Imagine being pumped up on adrenaline for days, weeks, or months. Not only will it impair your memory and brain processing, it will leave you unable to function in general. This is what people with PTSD suffer, but to a much higher degree.

Acute stress, on the other hand, is not something that will slide by unnoticed.

Acute stress is the sudden jolt of adrenaline you experience when someone cuts you off in traffic and you nearly crash, or you get into a heated argument. Incidentally, many opportunities for acute stress tend to occur in traffic situations. It might even be getting into a car accident. However, acute stress is momentary, temporary, and you can feel it and notice it. Intense bouts of acute stress can cause headaches, muscle tension, upset stomachs, or vomiting. This is when adrenaline is coursing through your veins trying to give you the alertness and strength you need for anything. If it persists and lasts for a longer period of time, it just may cross the threshold into chronic stress.

But the labels are unimportant. What's important is what happens to the memory processing systems when you are under any type of stress.

You can also think of the brain as simply being occupied with thoughts of stress and anxiety, so much so that it is unable to divert brainpower to memory and thinking clearly. This wouldn't be an inaccurate characterization of the role of stress. Stress can literally change your brain's structure and size, so it's something to devote a bit more attention to.

Make sure that the engine of your brain is running right when you need it. Try to eliminate or at least manage the stressors in your life, and make sure you aren't actually fulfilling the clinical definitions for depression, which is one of the most function-impairing conditions. Ask yourself what the major sources of anxiety are in your life.

They might be people, work, or even material objects. Whatever the case, make sure you are only doing what you need to and nothing unfairly on behalf of others.

Interestingly enough, intense stress can very occasionally have the opposite effect and create what are known as flashbulb memories, but we'll get to that in a later chapter.

Sleep

It has long been argued that specific modes of sleep are where memories are actually created. It is thought that the brain's structure is changed and synaptic connections are formed during sleep.

Indeed, studies have teased out the specifics of how memories are enhanced or stored during sleep. In a 2005 study, Professor Matthew Walker of Harvard University was able to compare fMRI scans of the brain while awake and sleep to see the different parts of the brain that were activated—where memory consolidation occurred. He found that people's cerebellums were far more active after a period of sleep between periods of learning, and this active was highly correlated with better learning and memory.

Professor Walker commented, "Sleep appears to play a key role in human development. At 12 months of age, infants are in an almost constant state of motor skill learning, coordinating their limbs and digits in a variety of routines. They have an immense amount of new material to consolidate and, consequently, this intensive period of learning may demand a great deal of sleep."

Specifically, rapid eye movement (REM) sleep is most important for memory consolidation and storage during sleep. There has been debate in recent years about just how important it is to memory, but sleep can also serve another purpose—we sleep to forget the unimportant facets of our day and filter them out so our memories can be more organized.

The Roles of Stress, Sleep, and Exercise

In 2003, research conducted at the University of Wisconsin-Madison hypothesized that neurons and synapses essentially worked and proliferated in overload during the day, and were pruned back during sleep so only the important things made it into longer-term memory. This implied that we sleep to literally forget certain parts of our day and have better-organized memory.

Sleep can serve many specific purposes on the brain and memory, but overall, the brain, like the body, needs rest and recovery. When you can provide the systems responsible for memory a reprieve overnight, it is simply likely they will continue to work better for you in the coming days.

Exercise

It might surprising to hear that physical exercise is just as good for your brain as it is for your muscles and bones, but it's been proven time and time again.

One particular study was conducted at Radboud University in the Netherlands. Male and female subjects took a memory test, then one third of them exercised immediately after the test, one third of them exercised four hours after the test, and the remaining third did not exercise after the test. The subjects were collected two days later to repeat the same memory test, and the group who exercised four hours after the initial test performed the best without fail. It appeared that exercise was effective in helping the brain stabilize and store the memory.

Other studies take the physiological angle and point to

the neurotransmitters and hormones that exercise releases and how they affected memory processes. Exercise is instrumental in the production of a brain protein called FNDC5, which eventually releases brain-derived neurotrophic factor (BDNF). BDNF has been shown to aid general brain functioning and memory processing by preserving existing brain cells, promoting new brain cells, and promoting overall brain growth. Human brains tend to shrink when we grow older, but exercise which creates BDNF can literally increase the size of your brain.

Your brain primarily uses glucose (what carbohydrates are converted into) for fuel, and when that is not available, it begins to use fat for fuel. It is when the brain starts to use fat for fuel that triggers BDNF creation. This is possibly behind the science of fasting and why low-carbohydrate diets have been shown to report high amounts of alertness and cognitive acuity as pleasant side-effects (Fond, 2012).

Your brain has the highest oxygen requirement of any organ in your body, up to 20% of your entire body's usage. When you can exercise and improve your cardiovascular systems and ensure that blood is pumping better through your arteries, you will have greater access to oxygen. It's the same with water—the brain is, on average, 70% composed of water, so exercise makes you more aware of hydration.

Exercise does have its limits, however. The best types of exercise are those that increase blood flow and burn fat. If exercise becomes too strenuous and difficult, then you begin to create stress, and you've already read how detrimental stress can be on your mental faculties. Overall, it appears that the maxim

The Roles of Stress, Sleep, and Exercise

of healthy body, healthy mind holds very true.

It's just another case of why we should have listened to our mothers more when were young. When we can avoid the stressors in our life, we can devote more mental bandwidth to that which matters. You wouldn't be great at studying for a test if your dog was missing, would you? We can better comprehend and understand difficult material when we have a full night's sleep. Finally, exercise is not only invigorating and important for giving you a mental break, but it can cause chemical changes in the brain that benefit your memory processes.

The brain is the engine of memory, and you have to be mindful of priming it for optimal performance.

4

MEMORY IMPROVEMENT METHODS PT. I

At this point in the book, we've examined the biology of memory, how and why it works, how we tend to forget and our how memory fails us, and even what contributes to the overall health and efficacy of memory.

It's a lot, and it is important knowledge. Understanding the basis of what you are trying to improve and influence can lead you to take an entirely different approach to it. But it's not exactly what you were looking for.

This is the first chapter where you just might find exactly what you were looking for when you picked up this book—memory techniques that make encoding, storage, and memory retrieval easier for our daily lives. You'll see that despite all of the reasons for forgetting, or the ways our brains can misfire or become under-nourished, there are many ways that people can retain huge amounts of information. It's helpful to think of each particular memory as a magnet. There are many ways of finding that particular magnet in the stores of your brain, from building an elaborate magnetic machine, to painting the magnet, to simply knowing how magnets work.

As a precursor to specific memory techniques, most of them are based on the principle of general rehearsal or giving information some type of significance which could bring up specific memories. Rehearsal is just what you think it is—it's when you recite something, review it, and read it to yourself over and over again to cement it into your memory. It's not the most elegant or effective method of committing something to memory, but it absolutely works.

The problem with rehearsal, otherwise known as rote memorization, is that it takes time and is the long way to memorization. Other techniques in this chapter are both shorter and easier—who doesn't want that? If you could spend less time studying for a test, and also end up retaining more, that's the best-case scenario.

Spaced Repetition

Spaced repetition is just what it sounds like.

In order to commit more to memory and retain information better, space out your rehearsal and exposure to it over as long a period as possible. In other words, you will remember something far better if you study it for one hour a day, versus 20 hours in one weekend. This goes for just about everything you could possibly learn. Additional research has shown that seeing something 20 times in one day is far less effective than seeing something 10 times over the course of seven days.

Spaced repetition makes more sense if you imagine your brain as a muscle. Muscles can't be exercised all the time and then put back to work with little to no recovery. Your brain needs time to make connections between concepts, create muscle memory, and generally become familiar with something. Sleep has been shown to be where neural connections are made, and it's not just mental. Synaptic connections are made in your brain and dendrites are stimulated.

Here's a look at what a schedule focused on spaced repetition might look like.

Monday at 10:00 AM—learn initial facts about Spanish history. You accumulate five pages of notes.

Monday at 8:00 PM—review notes about Spanish history, but don't just review passively. Make sure to try to recall the information from your own memory. Recalling is a much better way to processing information than simply re-reading and reviewing. This might only take 20 minutes.

Tuesday at 10:00 AM—try to recall the information without looking at your notes much. After you first try to actively recall as much as possible, go back through your notes to see what you missed and make note of what you need to pay closer attention to. This will probably take only 15 minutes.

Tuesday at 8:00 PM—review notes. This will take 10 minutes.

Wednesday at 4:00PM—try to independently recall the information again, and only look at your notes once you are done to see what else you have missed. This will take only 10 minutes. Make sure not to skip any steps.

Memory Improvement Methods Pt. I

Thursday at 6:00 PM—review notes. This will take 10 minutes.

Friday at 10:00 AM—active recall session. This will take 10 minutes.

Looking at this schedule, note that you are only studying an additional 75 minutes throughout the week, but you've managed to go through the entire lesson a whopping six additional times. Not only that, you've likely committed most of it to memory because you are using active recall instead of passively reviewing your notes.

You're ready for a test the next Monday. Actually, you're ready for a test by Friday afternoon. Spaced repetition gives your brain time to process concepts and make its own connections and leaps because of the repetition.

Think about what happens when you have repeated exposure to a concept. The first couple of exposures, you may not see anything new. As you get more familiar with it and stop going through the motions, you begin to examine it on a deeper level and think about the context surrounding it. You begin to relate it to other concepts or information, and you generally make sense of it below surface level.

All of this, of course, is designed to push information from your short-term memory into your long-term memory. That's why cramming, or studying at the last minute, isn't an effective means of learning. Very little tends to make it into long-term memory because of the lack of repetition and deeper analysis.

Just as an illustration of the applicability of spaced repetition, Paul Pimsleur discovered that for his audio-based language learning program, there were very specific pauses that led to increased learning. In other words, there were very specific intervals of time between the repetitions that showed better language learning and retention.

The intervals he discovered were: 5 seconds, 25 seconds, 2 minutes, 10 minutes, 1 hour, 5 hours, 1 day, 5 days, 25 days, 4 months, and 2 years. This shows the importance of repetition, especially soon after initial exposure.

Memories are more effectively created when they are processed and analyzed on a deeper level, because they form a vivid mental image versus a set of facts and descriptions that the brain filters as boring and useless.

Mnemonics

Mnemonics are another effective strategy for improving memory and retaining more information. You've probably used a mnemonic before—you just didn't know the name for it. Generally, a mnemonic device is something that helps organize a large amount of information into something that is more easily memorable—a set of cues to help you recall. As such, it can take a variety of forms.

The mnemonic device most commonly seen is an acronym, where the first letter might represent a word for each. FBI is an acronym for Federal Bureau of Investigation, which is a mouthful to remember. You can create acronyms for just about anything.

Here's an example of an acronym, where the first letters

of each word each represent a word: the colors of the rainbow are far more easily remembered as ROY G BIV **(red, orange, yellow, green, blue, indigo, violet)**. This acronym is helpful because instead of seven distinct colors, you only have to represent seven distinct letters—and you can also order the letters in a way that will make them even easier to remember. ROY G BIV can easily be someone's name, so to remember the seven colors of the rainbow, you now only have to remember someone's full name.

The acronym type of mnemonic is the easiest way to use it. Another way of making it easy to remember is to make the acronym a phrase.

For example, the classification system for organisms is far more easily remembered as Devoted King Philip Came Over For Good Soup **(domain, kingdom, phylum, class, order, family, genus, species)**.

The order of the planets of our solar system: My Very Easy Method: Just Say Understand Nelly **(Mercury, Venus, Earth, Mars, Jupiter, Saturn, Uranus, Neptune)**.

If you can create a mnemonic that has meaning or is a phrase on its own, that's even easier to remember. Also, the more vivid and outlandish the acronym or imagery, the better and easier it is to remember.

Another mnemonic device is to create a rhyme out of the information you want to remember. This is likely the only way you remember lyrics of many songs—you know the words that are close to it, and you know it must rhyme with them, so you can even remember them through process of elimination.

For example, do you remember the lyrics to the nursery rhyme, "Twinkle, Twinkle, Little Star"? The first line rhymes with the second, and the third line rhymes with the fourth. If you knew just the rhyming parts of first and third lines, you would probably be able to come up with the rest of it by filling in the blank:

Twinkle, twinkle, little **star**,
How we wonder what you are.
Up above the world so **high**,
Like a diamond in the sky.

"Star" rhymes with "are" and "high" rhymes with "sky"—it's not a stretch to think if you only remember "star" and "high," the rest might spring to mind immediately. Thus, you can create rhymes through poems or songs to make information stick in your brain more easily. You only have to remember a few key words, and you'll be able to fill in the blanks with the rest of the terms or concepts.

Create a Story

This is otherwise known as a narrative method. You are creating a story that happens to incorporate the information you want to memorize, because a story is easier to remember than a dry set of facts.

Consider the movie *Slumdog Millionaire*. The main character is lucky enough to appear on the Indian version of Who Wants to be a Millionaire?, and happens to know the answer to every trivia question. If he had been studying for the show, it's unlikely he would have come across all of these facts and committed them to memory. There simply would have been too much to remember.

However, he was able to remember the pieces of trivia because he had personal experiences with them in his life in some way. For example, he remembered the name of a song because he was forced to sing it as a child, and he remembered the name of an actor because he endured massive embarrassment and struggle to meet him. They were a part of the story of his life, and thus they were much easier to remember.

After all, aren't we more likely to associate songs with past significant others, even though they are no longer in the picture? We don't have to have such a tumultuous life to use a story to remember information, however. It's good enough for our purposes to just make up a story that has some logical flow that we are likely to remember.

Stories substitute a series of facts that are difficult to remember without ascribing them to something that is simpler and has personal meaning to you.

Here's an example of something that I've remembered for the past twelve years because of how it illustrated information so perfectly in my mind: Humans have two types of receptors in their eyes, rods and cones. One is for perceiving black and white, and the other is for perceiving color. Which is which?

Well, traffic cones are bright orange, while rods resemble the silver poles that hold up stop signs. Therefore, cones perceive color, and rods perceive black and white.

Improve Your Memory

What you're doing is drawing out the main elements of something and putting it into something you understand and remember. Put it into a context that is so obvious to you that all you have to do is be prompted.

Find something with one or two striking characteristics, then think about how it can relate to Spanish history and say, "It's similar to the Inquisition because …" If a story has a good guy and a bad guy, you can characterize them as the historical figures. You can think about them in terms of the difference between motorcycles and cars. A particular aspect might seem like the process of baking a cake. The end result may remind someone of how your mother treated you when you refused to come home for Christmas that one year.

A picture of a tree might remind you of the geography of a country because of the curves of the branches.

You can use players on your favorite baseball team to memorize the members of a country's government. Who resembles whom and why? You can use a song to remind you of a history lesson because the song is about rebuilding.

It's also this active analysis and application of a story, imagery, or metaphor to your information that further helps memory become solidified. You're searching to tie new information into existing information in an engaging manner. You might even remember the thought process more than the story or metaphor itself.

Memory Improvement Methods Pt. I

Peg Word Method

The peg word method involves substituting novel, difficult to remember information with already known, familiar information. As such, this method requires more work because you will have to learn a certain set of information first as your baseline.

There is one primary way the peg word method is used. It is known as the ***number/rhyme peg method***. This works when you assign each number from one to 10 a word that rhymes with it. For example:

One—sun
Two—screw
Three—spree
Four—door
Five—drive
Six—ticks
Seven—heaven
Eight—mate
Nine—stein
Ten—zen

In order for the peg word method to work, you will have to first memorize this list of rhymes—but it's inherently easier because they rhyme. Now that you have this baseline of knowledge to work with, you can use it to memorize 10 new pieces of information by using the rhymed words to make a story.

For example, let's say you want to memorize a list of

groceries: bread, milk, cheese, water, and eggs.

The first five rhymes are: sun, screw, spree, door, drive—these act as anchors and tell you where you are in your list.

A sample story regarding the grocery list would be:

A loaf of **bread** lays out in the **sun**, while a bottle of **milk** is popped with a metal **screw**. Nearby, a slice of **cheese** is on a shopping **spree**. He is going to hit a bottle of **water** with a **door**, and the king of the **eggs** are about to drive into the **countryside**.

So you've created a story with all sorts of wild and interesting imagery. All you have to do is go through the sequence in your mind and the grocery list will be much easier to remember. The peg word method works because you already know the basic structure of the story, and you likely already have it visualized. You have constructed a scene in your mind, and you are just filling in some blanks in that scene with new information. It's like putting a Post-It note on a photograph—you know the photograph already, and the new information sticks out and completes the overall scene.

The memory techniques in this chapter are largely about improving memory retrieval—that is, we know it's difficult to truly be able to recall all the information we want. However, the information is there, like a magnet, waiting to be detected by a metal detector. We are working on building metal detectors for specific information. The next chapter focuses more on the encoding phase—how we can intake information more powerfully and deeply.

5

MEMORY IMPROVEMENT METHODS PT. II

Still with me? Welcome to part two of memory improvement methods—in other words, likely the part of the book that is most important to you.

In the previous chapter, we covered a few methods on how to improve memory retrieval and make things stand out more in your memory. This chapter will focus a bit more on better encoding—how to make sure the information that passes through one ear doesn't just fly out the other.

Teach Others

The significance of teaching others to memorize and learn better has been well-documented. There are numerous studies to show the real-life effects, but it's perhaps the most helpful to start with the most popular representation of how teaching others is helpful—the Learning Pyramid.

The Learning Pyramid (NTL Institute) was created in the 1960s as a rough representation of the types of activities that help people learn and memorize better. Many people have questioned the accuracy of the pyramid, but I would argue that it's not meant to be taken as an exact number, but rather a guideline that demonstrates what really matters in retaining knowledge. The pyramid is as follows:

- You retain 5% when you hear a lecture
- 10% when you read
- 20% from audio-visual processing
- 30% from demonstrating [this and up are demonstration methods]
- 50% from group discussion [this and below are participatory methods]
- 75% from practice by doing
- 90% from teaching others

The exact numbers may not be that important, but the differences in style are telling. The middle few might differ for many people, but the ends of the spectrum are absolutely true. The more you proactively process and participate in the analysis of information, the better you will retain and remember it. The more passively you intake information without a second thought, the less you will retain and remember. Would you remember how to surf after surfing for two hours, or from watching a movie about surfing? Watching the movie is passive and doesn't make you participate or think in any meaningful way, but being in the water and surfing is going to teach you some very quick lessons.

Let's take two examples, one physical and one mental, to

Memory Improvement Methods Pt. II

see how this works in real life.

If you want to learn how to ski, you aren't going to remember much from a lecture or reading. You might remember the mechanics and why certain actions matter, but you won't actually be able to ski unless you do it. You demonstrate it for others, then receive immediate feedback, and you practice by doing so you can apply what you've learned. Obviously, for a physical act, we can see that effective memory is almost non-existent without moving down the spectrum toward active participation and analysis.

And now for the mental example.

If you want to remember the history of Spain, you might recall a good deal just from passively processing the information through a lecture or documentary. You could take notes, re-read your notes, watch a documentary on Spanish conquistadors and Christopher Columbus, and easily be considered well-read on the topic.

However, imagine how much more you would remember if you were to dissect with others the motivations of the Spanish Inquisition, or create a video to demonstrate just how Columbus sailed across the Atlantic Ocean. Further, imagine if you rehearsed a speech about Spanish history that was meant to teach your co-workers. Finally, imagine that your co-workers were all Spanish, so they were going to pepper you with questions you had to prepare for.

It's a different level of learning that occurs when you roll up your sleeves and really analyze a topic versus simply reading it. Remember, while the pyramid of learning isn't 100% accurate, it's accurate at the top and bottom levels, which create important distinctions in how much you retain and remember.

This is also why many researchers espouse the values of reading out loud and writing notes by hand versus typing. The more time we spend actively thinking about something, the more clearly it will become etched into our memory banks (Macpherson). The physical act of writing stimulates a different part of your brain from typing or merely thinking, meaning your brain is more active and involved when you write by hand.

The more time we spend breaking tasks down instead of doing them by habit, the more they are analyzed and examined, if even on a subconscious level. It's an unfortunate truth that most of us learn in the opposite way—at the top of the pyramid in passive, non-participatory methods that result in incredible information leakage.

The final benefit of teaching others, or more actively processing the information in front of us, is it forces us to see exactly what we do understand about it, and the information gaps that still remain. For example, if you want to teach someone about why the sky is blue, you might begin with speaking about how the sky reflects the ocean, but is that true or just a simplified explanation you've heard since you were young? And why wouldn't the sky reflect mountains and plains? You might realize that you actually don't know anything about why the sky is blue, and you will realize your information gap as a result of simply trying to explain a concept to someone.

Use Your Senses

Most people tend to think of memory as something that starts with just your eyes or ears. But that would be drastically shortchanging how your five senses work together to process information and make use of it.

For example, what happens if you were to discover and smell an old bottle of perfume or cologne that a past significant other used? If you came across a restaurant that smelled like your grandmother's house when she cooked? Moreover, what does smelling fresh laundry make you think of?

Any of these smells are likely to create a flood of memories.

Why does this happen? It's clear that our memories are not dependent on our senses of sight or hearing alone.

The sense of smell is highly tied to memories—in fact, each of your five senses can contribute to memory formation (Fields, 2012). Exposure to sight, taste, sound, touch, and smell can all serve as triggers for memories, and the more senses you can involve in creating a particular memory, the more deeply it will be embedded into your memory. This is why hearing a certain song, or feeling the texture of a table, can take you to a very specific point in time.

Just being in a certain environment, we take in everything on a subconscious level using our senses. Most of it is simply discarded because it's not seen as important enough to remember. But the information is in us somewhere, and if you can focus on associating information with your other senses, it gives your memory three more associations to draw upon.

Improve Your Memory

Let's momentarily think of a particular memory as a five-piece jigsaw puzzle. If you *see* something that reminds you of it, you still only have one part of the puzzle—you might not be able to decipher or recall it. But if you see something and also smell something that reminds you of the memory, you are going to have a much better chance of recall. Of course, this means if you can have a memory that involves all five of your senses, all five pieces of the jigsaw puzzle will be present and it's likely you will recall it easily.

Smell, in particular, is more powerful in triggering memories because its positioning in the brain is physically closest to the hippocampus, where memories are processed. Spanish psychologist Silvia Alava found that people remember 35% of what they smell versus 5% of what they see. That's why we are drawn into bouts of nostalgia and past events when we encounter certain smells. The smell associations are so strong that they often also evoke memories of emotions, not mere events.

In other words, to memorize more, always try to involve as many senses as possible. This might not always be practical, but you can typically involve at least two senses. Instead of reading something to yourself, read it out loud and try to memorize the texture of book's cover. Instead of listening to something, write it down so you can process it visually and light a scented candle so you can latch your sense of smell to something. You are creating more triggers for your memory recall at a later point in time.

For an illustration on some semi-practical suggestions:

suppose you are sitting in a classroom while you are studying for a test on the Spanish Inquisition. For each date or name, you might try to associate it with a few senses:

Sight: Try to associate the information with a painting on the wall.

Sound: Listen to specific songs for specific parts of the information.

Touch: Process the feeling of the desk you are sitting at.

Taste: Have different pieces of gum available.

Smell: Smell your backpack.

The Zeigarnik Effect

The Zeigarnik Effect is a psychological phenomenon stating that people tend to remember information better when it the information is perceived to be somehow incomplete or interrupted.

The Zeigarnik Effect was discovered by psychologist Bluma Zeigarnik, who noticed that waiters in restaurants always remembered unpaid orders far better than paid orders. The waiters could recite what was ordered on a table that hadn't yet paid, yet after the payment was received, the order was essentially evacuated from his brain.

You only have to look at the habit of television shows and movies using cliffhangers to understand this in a pinch. When a narrative is stopped right in the middle, it causes an emotional impact that creates mental fixation. Or you will have pristine memory of a particular problem at work if it isn't yet resolved.

When something is unfinished, it's like there is still a Post-It in our brain telling us to complete it. It's a tiny mental itch you want to scratch—and the itch doesn't go away until you complete the information, so you keep feeling the itch and focusing on it in the meantime. We rehearse it continually to make sure we don't forget it, though we might not even be sure why.

This is the feeling that you walked into a room to accomplish something, or something is on the tip of your tongue. Psychologist Kurt Lewin characterized it as a task-specific tension, which creates alertness and focus as a result of the tension. However, once the task is completed, the tension is relieved and the focus is removed from the task completely. The brain gets a break, essentially. If you interrupt or make information incomplete, you are maintaining perpetual, subconscious tension about that information.

Therefore, the Zeigarnik Effect helps your memory when you can interrupt yourself and create an itch in your brain about the information which will cause subconscious (or conscious) fixation on it. Zeigarnik specifically found that students remembered material better when they took breaks to partake in unrelated activities.

We are lured to information, and even tasks, if they feel incomplete. For example, if you see a cabinet door hanging open, you will probably feel a compulsion to close it. Similarly, if you see a sentence half-written or annotated in your notes, you will probably feel a compulsion to finish it.

To fully utilize the counterintuitive Zeigarnik Effect for

memory improvement, it's not just a matter of interrupting your own studies. It's a matter of:

1. Interrupting strategically.
2. Leaving unfinished tasks for yourself.

Interrupting strategically utilizes the Zeigarnik Effect by creating a cliffhanger for yourself. Imagine reading a story until just before the ending or resolution. That's what you can do with retaining information—consume information until right before the conclusion, then move to something else temporarily. When you come back and complete the information, you will retain more of it because it's been simmering in your mind for the entire interruption.

Leaving unfinished tasks for yourself utilizes the Zeigarnik Effect because you will feel compelled to finish it, and you will have been processing it in your subconscious the entire time.

Primary and Recency

The Primary and Recency Effects are well-known psychological phenomenon which states that we tend to remember the first (primacy) and last (recency) items in a list as opposed to objects that are in the middle, regardless of actual importance.

For instance, the following is a list of items to pack for a trip:

- Toothbrush
- Socks

- Underwear
- Diabetes medicine
- Pens
- Pencil
- Erasers
- Belt

The Primacy Effect states that out of the list, the easiest item to remember will be the toothbrush. The Recency Effect (Miller) states that out of the list, the easiest item to remember will be the belt. Are either of those the most important items on that list? Absolutely not, but let's investigate why this happens.

Primacy tends to happen because we have implicit assumptions about the beginnings of lists holding greater significance or importance, so we naturally tend to focus our attention there. Primacy also capitalizes on when people are still paying attention. Imagine hearing the aforementioned list read out loud. You aren't going to want to pay attention for much longer than a few items, so the beginning will be where you aren't yet starting to daydream or lose focus. Finally, when we review lists or study our notes, we tend to always start at the beginning and work our way back—starting on page one and going in order until you reach the last page. Of course, we don't always reach the last page each time we review information, which means we are likely to read information on page one to page five more frequently.

Recency tends to happen because we assume that the ends of a list have implicit importance, and also because it is simply the information we hear the most recently, and thus it is fresher in our memories. Our short-term memory (the Post-It note) can't handle so much information, so it naturally zeroes in on what it assumes is important or easier to remember.

These two effects should influence how you view lists of information for optimal memorization. Avoid the middle, and put the key items at the beginning and end. An effective way to do this is to open and close each list or set of information with a summary of key points that may also be contained in the middle, but overlooked. Also seek to chunk information as the first and last item on a list so you can take advantage of these effects.

You can also use a mnemonic as your first and last items to make sure you get a larger breadth of information embedded in your memory, or continually re-write and shift lists into different orders so each item can eventually benefit from these effects.

6

MEMORY IMPROVEMENT METHODS PT. III

Welcome to the final chapter on memory improvement methods—other chapters are devoted to single methods, so maybe it's a bit of a misnomer. There's plenty more for you after this chapter, don't worry. Here, we'll explore the brain's tendency to fixate on visual imagery above all else, and the discoveries that led to the importance of the concept of chunking.

The Von Restorff Effect

The Von Restorff Effect is the proposition that we remember better what is distinctive, notable, or standing out in some way. The initial discovery of this effect was studied by Hedwig Von Restorff in 1933. Our attention is essentially enhanced by the distinct and noteworthy, which helps memory and retention.

For example, which of the following will be easiest to remember from this list:

Memory Improvement Methods Pt. III

- Dog
- Puppy
- Cat
- Kitten
- Zombie jet pilot
- Duck
- Duckling

I'll take a stab in the dark and guess that you will remember the zombie jet pilot the easiest. That is because everything else appears to follow a pattern, and the zombie jet pilot stands out immensely. It is distinctive by itself and within the rest of the information, and as such, is more easily embedded into our memory banks. It is distinct both by itself and in relation to everything around it.

You only need to take a look at any advertisement, book cover, billboard, or sign to see the Von Restorff Effect in action. Really, anything that is designed to capture attention, send a message, or sell. All marketing, from movie posters to brand logos are based at least in part on the Von Restorff Effect, whether the advertising teams know it or not. This is especially true in the modern age, where we are bombarded on a daily basis for our attention by corporate entities. He who is most distinct, outlandish, or absurd typically wins the battle for your attention, and thus better chance of accessing your memory.

Can you remember any commercials you've seen recently? Now, are any of those commercials boring or generic? No, you probably recalled commercials that were absurd and notable in some way, from a catchy jingle, to a funny premise, to exciting visual effects. Suppose you are in a grocery store and you want to buy peanut butter. These days, you'll be choosing between at least eight brands. You are probably going to be drawn immediately to brands that use bright and vivid packaging, and you'll remember them after you go to the next aisle. This is no mistake.

The premise of the Von Restorff Effect is pretty understandable, but how can you use this in your daily studies, or when you want to memorize people's names more effectively?

Using Visualization of Absurd Mental Imagery

When you can combine specific pieces of information with absurd mental imagery, you will give your memory a boost due to the combination of the Von Restorff Effect and images that capitalize on the brain's tendency to remember images more easily than information. In fact, memory has been said to be strongest visually (Burmark). So you are bridging the gap and turning information into images when you create associations, and cementing it when you make the associations absurd.

Information by itself can be difficult to make distinct or noteworthy, so attaching visual imagery to it is an easy way to do that. This can be particularly effective for names, because names by themselves don't typically provide any visual imagery unless the name is something like Autumn or Summer.

Let's take the name Richard (and not Dick), which isn't inherently descriptive or visual. You need to connect the name Richard to something because in a vacuum, you are just depending on the word Richard to stick in your memory, which is unreliable. How would you utilize the Von Restorff Effect along with distinct visual imagery?

Richard has two syllables, so you can use two pieces of imagery.

Rich = a wealthy man swimming in a pool of golden coins.

Herd = a crazy shepherd running around a flock of sheep that are singing "Happy Birthday."

Richard also happens to have black hair, so the images associated with Rich and Herd will take on a black tinge, as well as have black hair themselves, including black sheep. Therefore, when you are struggling to remember someone's name, this entire scene with the sheep and shepherd will likely pop up in your mind first, and is much easier to extract meaning from. It is rife with clues that you left for yourself, whereas just trying to remember "Richard" leads to a binary yes or no outcome.

Two steps occurred: First, you would come up with absurd visual imagery to be associated with someone's name, and second, you would connect the imagery to something about the person's appearance. Utilizing the Von Restorff Effect, it's quite easy to remember the scene of a wealthy man swimming in a pool of coins while a shepherd is attempting to calm a flock of black sheep—it's far more information than just hearing "Richard."

Since visuals are so much more easily taken into memory, you'll want to create distinct visual imagery to associate with dates, locations, times, and anything else you want to remember.

For example, suppose you parked your car at the intersection of Oak and Maple. A visual that would help you remember the intersection is to conjure an image of a knight with a large "O" on his shield fighting a knight with a large "M" on his shield, but they are both riding dogs.

Suppose you want to remember the date March 19, 2000. You can represent that as 3, 19, 2000. What mental image could you construct to include those three numbers?

Suppose you want to remember Spanish vocabulary words—*ventana*, which is Spanish for window. What mental image could you construct to make you remember what *ventana* means (the more vivid and absurd, the better)? You might imagine a window covered with metal vents look like they are meant to keep people from breaking into them, or extremely rusty metal vents that are jagged and have pieces of human flesh hanging from them. The list is endless. Assign fascinating imagery to things, and you will take advantage of how your brain prefers to store information.

Drawing

Drawing accomplishes the same effect that visual imagery and the Von Restorff Effect have. The brain more easily stores visual images, and the act of drawing them aids memory by anchoring information to that image. Again, information by itself is difficult to recall alone, but if you associate an image with it, you will have many more cues for recall.

Researchers led by Jeffrey Wammes found that when

subjects drew the words they were supposed to memorize, they had a significantly higher rate of recall than those who just read or thought about the words. They were up to twice as effective in their recall. Not only is drawing taking advantage of the brain's penchant for visual imagery (it's easier to remember a picture of an interesting gate with 1070 emblazoned on it than the number 1070 by itself), but it also introduces another layer of active participation where you are interacting with the information, and thus remembering it because you were actually using it to some degree.

The latter is what psychologists dub a deeper level of processing, and it is exactly what the Learning Pyramid is based on. Recall that the more participatory and active the manipulation of the information was, the better it was retained and committed to memory; whereas the more passively you take in information, the less of an imprint it makes and the more easily it will be forgotten.

Chunking

Chunking is a memory technique you may have heard of before, but there is quite a bit of research into why and how chunking works.

Chunking is the act of taking multiple pieces of information and combining them into fewer pieces of information, which is obviously easier to memorize. Mnemonics are an example of chunking, as are acronyms. A simple example is of a telephone number. If you want to memorize a telephone number, it's difficult to memorize seven independent numbers. However, you could create two three-digit numbers and a single-digit number, which is actually easier for your brain to process. 1234567 would become 123-456-7.

Chunking came about because of the discovery of *Miller's Magic Number 7*—a discovery made in 1956 by George Miller. He proclaimed that most people can store between five and nine pieces of information in their short-term memory, for an average of seven items, which accounts for the name.

However, what constitutes a piece of information can vary widely. Therefore, chunking information together can greatly increase what we hold in our short-term memory and make us far more effective. It's more accurate to say that we can hold five to nine *chunks* of information in our short-term memory at a time. As you might recall from the first chapters of this book, short-term memory has limited capacity, and chunking serves to cram as much information inside that limited capacity as possible.

Another way to think about chunking is to create one meaningful piece of information from multiple pieces of information. Whatever list or set of information you are analyzing or trying to commit to memory, attempt to chunk it down into anywhere from five to nine pieces of information. This won't just make you analyze the information with a more critical eye; it will also take advantage of Miller's Magic Number 7 and feed information to your brain in a way it can handle.

If you have two shopping lists that are represented by the mnemonics TREN and TABM, that's eight pieces of information that are condensed into only two chunks. Chunking allows you to know the limits of your memory and optimize your information to suit those limits. Some of us might be able to hold nine chunks of information in our short-term memory, but whenever possible, use mnemonic and memory devices to make life easy for your short-term memory.

The Major System

The Major System is similar to the peg word method as mentioned in an earlier chapter. It's best used for memorizing numbers. It's a great technique for memory, but it does require first memorizing the following sets of numbers and sounds they are associated with:

- 1-t
- 2-n
- 3-m
- 4-r
- 5-l
- 6-sh/j
- 7-k/g
- 8-v/f
- 9-p/b
- 0-c/s

The reason these sounds were chosen is because they represent the vast majority of sounds in the English language, close enough to all of them so you will be able to figure out words phonetically. The idea is that, again, visual imagery is easier to remember than dry numbers without any context, so you would take a large string of numbers and then convert it into letters and words according to the Major System.

Let's suppose your overall goal is to memorize the number 104,967.

According to the Major System, this would convert into the string of letters: TSRPSJG. This is currently gibberish and no easier to remember than the numbers, but you would make a phrase out of the letters that you are left with. TSRPSJG could become the phrase "Taser Pass Jig." TSRPSJG can become anything you want, as long as you can fit the phrase and words around the sounds of the numbers. You can see how this would be easier to remember—and because the sounds are still preserved in the phrase, you can easily convert "Taser Pass Jig" back into the number 104,967.

Memorizing the sounds of the Major System only takes a few days—from there, you are only limited by your sense of creative imagery and phrasing.

Meditate

Even though meditation seems like a technique that has debatable and ambiguous benefits, it's been proven multiple times to aid clarity of thought, improve memory, and reduce overall stress—recall how damaging stress can be on the size of the brain, and you'll see why this concept is so important.

Meditation is the act of simply stopping the noise in your

mind. It involves sitting still and quiet, clearing your mind, and concentrating on a singular thought, sound, or sentence. Some might see it as relaxing, and others might see it as pushing the mind to its limits.

Why does this improve memory and aid clarity of thought? Actually, there are a range of reasons.

- Lower stress and anxiety.
- Training better focus and concentration.
- Simply taking a mental break to refresh.
- Neurochemical changes related to serotonin and dopamine, known as pleasure neurotransmitters.

Whatever the most important reason for you, meditation can have a huge effect on your memory. You are putting your brain into a position where it can perform at its best. Sometimes this can be more important than having the best mnemonics or mastering the Major System. A couple of additional hours of sleep or playtime might amount to an increase in memory comparable to hours of study, simply because your brain is fresher.

Meditation can be hard to wrap your mind around because many people try to make it more complex than it really is. Here's a short primer on the meditation I perform a few times a week to clear my mind. It's stunning in its simplicity.

Step one: Sit in a dark, quiet space. I prefer to sit on the ground next to a wall because it's comfortable enough, yet not so comfortable that I might fall asleep. This is personal preference. Just make sure you are comfortable and it's a position you will find acceptable and where you won't feel an imminent cramp.

Step two: Set an alarm. To start, 5 minutes might be more than enough for you.

Step three: Focus on your breathing. When I say this, I mean to attempt to think about literally nothing else besides your breath. There is only the inhale and exhale, and that should be what you occupies your mind. The end goal is actually to have a completely blank mind, but that's difficult to start with. You can use visual imagery at first, if it helps. Something peaceful, like the waves on a beach, could help keep your mind from wandering. Others repeat a mantra or word to themselves. This is all with the goal of clearing your mind and focusing only on your breathing. Take deep breaths and focus on where one breath begins and another one ends.

Create a blank slate for your mind. There are only three real steps, at least as a beginner. Hopefully, this context shows what why meditation can be so helpful. Many of us operate on high levels of subconscious stress or are just plain bad at focusing. When you can work on both of these issues simultaneously, your memory can't help but improve.

What follows next are two in-depth and detailed descriptions of memory techniques. For most of the memory techniques in parts I-III, once you know them, you can immediately use them. They're just devices for memory. The next two techniques are anything but, as you'll see.

7

THE MEMORY PALACE TECHNIQUE

One of the most famous memory techniques is known as the method of loci, but more commonly known as the memory palace. This is actually a technique that was invented over 2000 years ago in ancient Greece by Simonides of Ceos. It was used to allow ancient Greek and Roman speakers to present for hours without requiring notes or manuscripts.

That's a time when oration, rhetoric, and presentation became an art form, so as you can imagine, it was imperative to be able to speak from memory and without aid. Today, it's what nearly all of the world's memory champions and winners of memory contests use as one of their primary tools. It's based on the premise that even if we haven't physically been somewhere in a while, we remember routes and locations easily.

The memory palace, in a nutshell, works when you visualize yourself walking through a familiar location, such as your house, a palace, or your neighborhood. You've placed items or pieces or information along your path so that when you visualize walking through your palace, you can become reminded of the information as you walk by. If you are giving a speech, you will mentally walk through your palace and see each turn and become reminded of their next topic. It sounds so simple and easy that it almost seems like fiction, but it's truly not. You don't have to become a master of the memory palace for it to work wonders for your memory capacity.

There are usually a few layers of disbelief when it comes to using a memory palace.

First, it seems difficult to be able to visualize walking through your home in such great detail. It's easier than you think, and you could probably do it right now.

Second, it seems difficult to come up with specific details about each room or turn in your house. Again, that is also easier than you think. You instinctually know what's in your bathroom just because it's a bathroom, and you could recall more specific details with just a bit of thought.

Finally, it seems like a huge leap to be able to visualize your home and suddenly remember information. That, we'll get to.

Your Palace

The first step to the memory palace technique is to define your palace. Choose the location you are going to use, and then define the route you will take through it. It must be intimately familiar to you, and the path you choose must be easy and natural to follow—that is, if you were to forget the route, it's the one you would pick anyway because of the natural flow of the location.

The Memory Palace Technique

For that reason, it's not always best to choose your own home—it might be labyrinthine or not have a clear flow. Some people like to use office buildings or even museums, because there is a clear order of what to see and where to go. Of course, those must be balanced with familiarity.

Make sure there are at least a few rooms that you will pass through, and within each room, a few distinct items.

In the end, what's most important about the palace is that you will be able to see it clearly in your head when you are tired or under duress. With enough practice, you can transform just about any location into your palace.

The Cues

A memory palace is not just the palace itself; the important part is to have cues that present themselves clearly along your path.

For example, you might indeed make your own home your memory palace. Suppose your home has a hallway, a kitchen, a bedroom, and a bathroom. What are three specific items you would expect to see, without fail, in each of those locations or rooms?

Hallway: shoes, doorknob, umbrella
Kitchen: oven, microwave, pots
Bedroom: bed, tissues, teddy bear
Bathroom: toothpaste, shower gel, toilet plunger

A couple of those elements might be personal, but largely, they are universal. They are also likely to be very vivid—as in, you have a very clear idea of what they look like in your home. You know the colors of the shoes near your front door, and which pairs you wear often and which you tend to ignore. You know how the doorknob feels and the resistance it gives when you turn it. You can see how wet or dusty your umbrella is, depending on the amount of usage.

Point being, these are all very concrete items you can easily visualize. You can see them in high detail, and they even stick out in the location because of their detail. Of course, we learned about the Von Restorff Effect last chapter, so these items will be far easier to remember if they are distinct, funny, odd, or even lewd. This means you can add small flourishes or details to these items that will make them stand out, such as an umbrella shaped like a phallus, shoes overflowing with odor, a doorknob that doubles as a peephole into a topless cabaret—you get the idea.

Note that there are only three items in each location or room. Recall Miller's Magic Number 7—we don't want to tax that or come near the limit, so I would recommend having an upper limit or four or five items in each room. Anything more than that, and your short-term memory will likely struggle. In our current path through our home is 12 items, and they are in a certain order because of how you enter your home and walk inside. You'll first go through the hallway, pass the kitchen, pass the bedroom, then pass the bathroom in a straight line. It's a logical flow.

Each of these 12 items will be cues for you to use, so it's important to be know them like the back of your hand.

The Memory Palace Technique

Commit your route to memory however you want. You can start by drawing out your path through your memory palace, saying everything out loud, putting the items on flashcards assigned to the certain locations, or just repeat them through rote repetition. You are developing your capacity for visualization here, which is likely not something you've flexed much in the past. This memory palace and the associated route and items will be something you can use for an infinite number of information to remember. It will be the foundation for the next step.

Associate

Now that you've moved into your palace and made it your home, we can put it to use.

The memory palace technique uses a slightly different version of the peg word method we covered earlier. There, we used words as cues that were associated with numbers. Here, we are using each item in our home as a peg, and we are combining it with a piece of information you want to memorize.

In other words, you will be combining each new piece of information with an item in your home. You will create a Frankenstein item from putting the two together, and you will eventually be able to see that item when you walk through your castle. Visual imagery is best remembered when it is unusual or absurd. If it's boring, you won't remember it, and you'll only remember the item you've placed in your home, such as the shoes or umbrella. That, of course, is unhelpful.

So, for example, you want to a shopping list that consists

of: bread, milk, yogurt, chicken, water, and gum. It doesn't need to be in any order, but let's look back at the palace and items we've defined.

> Hallway: shoes, doorknob, umbrella
> Kitchen: oven, microwave, pots
> Bedroom: bed, tissues, teddy bear
> Bathroom: toothpaste, shower gel, toilet plunger

There are only six items on the shopping list, so only the following items in the memory palace are required: shoes, doorknob, umbrella, oven, microwave, pots. Now, let's match them up with the shopping list:

> Shoes: bread
> Doorknob: milk
> Umbrella: yogurt
> Oven: chicken
> Microwave: water
> Pots: gum

At this point, we must combine the two concepts into memorable imagery so you will have a great reminder of your shopping list as you walk through the memory palace. Think of it as drawing on the item in the memory palace to remind you of the shopping list.

Shoes + bread = A rich man wearing shoes made out of bread because they are the new silly trend set by the Kardashians, and the bread has butter and jam, which cost extra. The man is wearing a tuxedo, but shoes made out of plain white bread.

The Memory Palace Technique

Doorknob + milk = A pot of milk that kids use for "bobbing for doorknobs" instead of bobbing for apples during Halloween. The doorknobs are bouncing up and down amongst the waves of milk as kids try to pick them up with their teeth.

Umbrella + yogurt = You're standing outside and it's raining yogurt, and you are using an umbrella to keep you dry. All the cars around you are crashing, but the yogurt keeps coming. Also, the umbrella is made of granola and berries.

Oven + chicken = It's a chicken composed out of ovens like a giant robot made out of smaller, individual robots. When the robot moves, it squawks like a rooster crowing at dawn. Each feather is a button of an oven.

And so on. It requires a bit of creativity, but as with all things we repeat and practice, it gets easier with time, and you will find your own style that makes memorization even easier and more predictable.

When you open the door to your memory palace, the first thing you are going to see is your hallway which contains shoes, a doorknob, and an umbrella. Except now, instead of seeing just those items, you are seeing the visual combinations we created above. Keep walking and follow the route in your memory palace, and you know what to do. The process doesn't change, and neither does the route. The only thing that changes is what you mentally associate with the items in your memory palace.

The memory palace technique is difficult if it's new to you and you don't have your palace memorized with sufficient detail. But when you get better, a curious thing will happen: the items you are trying to memorize will instantly spring into your mind as you look at the objects along your memory palace route. It's what happens when you create such strong and powerful visual imagery—and another demonstration of the fact that the brain literally devotes a larger portion to sight than any other sense.

It truly does become as easy as taking a mental stroll through your home. The hard part is coming up with visual combinations, but that's something you will improve with over time. Eventually, your filters will come down, and you will realize that the more outlandish and inappropriate your visual combinations are, the easier they are to conceive of and the easier they are to remember. There's a reason the ancient Greeks and Romans used this technique!

8

DEVELOPING PHOTOGRAPHIC MEMORY

We've all heard the myth of the genius who can look at a poster, nature scene, or even book, and then with 100% accurately recite what they saw. If it's a poster, they can talk about all the details and colors. If it's a nature scene, they'll remember every tree, deer, and bird flying in the sky. If it's a book, then they will literally be able to read the book from their memory, treating the words that they glimpsed as a mental script.

Sounds a bit fantastical and too good to be true, especially when presented with promises that you too could achieve this.

Unfortunately, it is likely too good to be true. Too much evidence over the years has shown that it's almost impossible to recall visual images with 100% accuracy in a manner that you could call photographic. That, combined with the fact that there have been few, if any, demonstrations of photographic memory have led most people to admit defeat in the pursuit of true photographic memory.

In a sense, it's somewhat shocking that the ability for true photographic memory hasn't been documented to exist. People are capable of incredible memory capacities and tricks:

- People can recite pi to thousands of digits.
- Chess masters can memorize dozens of moves for each permutation of the board they are looking at.
- Gamblers can memorize the cards that have already been dealt out of multiple decks.

Why not photographic memory? Good question, but it's a question that is yet unanswered.

The closest we have come to true photographic memory that treats our visual brain like a printout is what is known as *eidetic memory* (Searleman). Eidetic roughly means "amazingly detailed and vivid recall of images" in Greek. Those with eidetic memory, after being shown a novel image for 30 seconds, can describe the image with high detail and accuracy, yet not 100% in either dimension. They see, process, and memorize the images, but the outcome can't be called truly photographic because then they would report with 100% accuracy, and the memories wouldn't fade after only a few minutes.

For example, they'll be able to look at a page and read most of it back to you, with 90% accuracy after studying it for a short period of time.

However, even this level of photographic memory has been disputed many times—the recall is often attributed to a combination of luck and reconstruction because new details and inaccuracies occur (Lilienfeld). Someone could very well have an exceptional memory and be able to remember individual pieces of data, but not through revisiting an image saved in their brain.

There are a few other types of exceptional memory, but they unfortunately also haven't been shown to confirm the existence of photographic memory.

Hyperthymesia

Hyperthymesia is when you can remember with an abnormal amount of detail their life experiences. Notably, it only applies to their autobiographical memory. What they had for lunch yesterday, last week, and even last year are things someone with hyperthymesia would be able to easily recall.

A spectacular subject named "AJ" was discovered and studied, and she reported recalling every single day of her life from when she was 14 years old (Parker). She wasn't able to recall specific things in detail, but she knew what happened to her and what she was involved in. For example, when asked about specific dates, her replies were as follows:

April 3, 1980?—"I see it. Spring break. Passover, I went to that week. I was on Spring Break. I see the week."

July 1, 1986?—"I see it all, that day, that month, that summer. Tuesday. Went with (friend's name) to (restaurant name)."

October 3, 1987?—"That was a Saturday. Hung out at the apartment all weekend, wearing a sling—hurt my elbow."

April 27, 1994?—"That was Wednesday. I was down in Florida ... to come down and say goodbye to my grandmother, who they all thought was dying, but she ended up living. My dad and my mom went to New York for a wedding. This was also the weekend Nixon died."

When AJ's brain was scanned and analyzed, the parts of her brain typically associated seemed normal, but she had other markers that made her brain resemble someone with obsessive-compulsive disorder. So was her extreme and exceptional memory the result of innate ability, or someone who was obsessed with cataloguing the details of her personal life?

Though this sounds like it would be a handy ability, it also means that AJ wouldn't be able to forget anything negative that happened; an insult from three years ago might still ring in her ears as powerfully as the day she first heard it. Her emotions also likely wouldn't be forgotten, and she would feel forever stuck between the past and the present. What would her mood depend on—a memory from last year, or the carnival she is currently at?

Indeed, additional testing by other researchers at the University of California, Irvine have shown that AJ's abilities affects other aspects of how she thinks (McGaugh). They tested various aspects of memorization, IQ, and executive function (essentially, the ability to focus and maintain attention), and of course, she did well on the memory portions. However, AJ's scores on executive function were very low. In other words, she wasn't good at focusing on singular tasks and paying attention for extended periods of time. Instead, she was likely focused on trying to notice and encode details regarding her surroundings.

Her brain was constantly distracted by thoughts of the past and taking in her environment, keeping her spectacularly out of the present and unable to make plans. Everything was a reminder of something in AJ's past, and she exhibited a natural inability to separate or ignore that.

Hyperthysemia has been shown to exist, but not without some cost to the wielder of this power.

Savants

The notion of the savant was popularized in the 1988 movie *Rain Man*, starring Tom Cruise and Dustin Hoffman.

In the movie, Dustin Hoffman plays a savant who is socially stunted and developmentally challenged (in the way that the autism spectrum creates), yet incredibly gifted with specific mental and memory abilities. A savant is one who possess developmental delays, yet shows incredible gifts in particular and specific areas—there are only 32 confirmed savants as of the time of the publication of this book.

Rain Man was based on the real-life story of savant Kim Peek, although he wasn't autistic in real life. Kim Peek's memory was the stuff of legend. He was able to remember everything he had ever read in his life, and could simultaneously read two books at once—one book with one eye each. More than that, he would retain up to 98% of what he had read. He became a walking encyclopedia and map, and could also name the day of the week if you gave him any date in history.

Peek didn't suffer from autism, but he didn't have a corpus

callosum in his brain, which is the membrane that literally connects the left and right hemispheres of the brain. This was possibly why Peek was able to simultaneously read two books. Obviously, savantism is a type of memory ability that is not reproducible, and it seems like something that came from science fiction first, rather than a real life event that inspired a movie. Kim Peek reportedly read over 10,000 books in his life, and with a recall rate of 98%, it's staggering to imagine.

Yet this doesn't get us any closer to photographic memory, either. We might have to come to grips that it simply doesn't exist. We can, however, train eidetic memory to where you can improve your memory in a practical sense for everyday application.

The Military Method

One urban legend is that specialized branches of various armed forces around the world possess eidetic memory on some level. Presumably, this is so they don't have to carry a camera around with them, and they can memorize the secret nuclear plans they find.

Whatever the case, the military method of training eidetic memory has indeed been shown to improve recall. The only caveat is that it will take at least a few weeks to improve and master, and you must practice is on a very consistent basis. And once you stop practicing it, many of the gains vanish.

Step one: Put yourself into a dark room free of distraction. Make it as dark as possible. If you have windows, put blackout curtains over them. Pitch black is preferable. The room must have a bright light inside—preferably a desk lamp that you can move around and focus on specific spots. A lamp you can hold and move also means you will be more comfortable waiting for your eyes to adjust to the dark.

Step two: Get a piece of paper and cut a rectangle out of the middle around the three inches high and five inches wide. You might have to start with a smaller section, if you find that this hole is too large.

Step three: Whatever you are trying to form a mental image of, whether it is a book or a painting, put it under the paper with the rectangular hole so only part of it is showing. You are going to focus only on that part that shows through the hole, and nothing else on the page, or even in the room—that's why having a room that can be dark is important. Adjust yourself so when you open and close your eyes, you can focus on the book or painting immediately.

Step four: Turn off the light and sit for a few minutes, or as long as it takes for your eyes to adjust fully to the dark. This could be up to five minutes. As soon as that happens, flip the light on for a second, and as soon as your eyes focus on your book or painting, flip the lights off. You should have a visual imprint of the information burned into your eyes. It won't stay too long, at first. This isn't exactly the information itself, rather an image of the information manipulated by how your eyes process light.

Step five: When the visual imprint fades from the back of your eyelids, repeat step four. Flip the light on, focus on the information, then flip the light off again. Repeat this process until you can build a strong enough visual image to recall nearly everything that is there. The more you do this, the clearer your image will be, and the longer it will last in your mind.

This is going to result in your feeling a bit silly the first few times, but various reports have indicated that repeating this process for 15 minutes a day for a period of 30 days will grant you near-eidetic powers—albeit on a limited and temporary basis. At that point, it becomes more habitual and ingrained in your brain's behavior, though this is disputable.

Overall, photographic memory is a myth until proven otherwise, but there are definitely other ways to improve your memory so you can recall more from a single glimpse, which is really the goal. Anecdotally, the military method worked for me, but it grows tedious after the first two weeks. However, once you stop, it is clear that your visual memory starts to function differently. There aren't any peer-reviewed studies on the effectiveness of the military method, but if one thing is sure, it's that the brain processes images faster subconsciously and subliminally than we consciously realize (Hassain), so we can be extracting far more from a single glimpse than we might know.

9

PHENOMENA OF MEMORY

Memory is full of interesting phenomena, partially because it's not 100% clearly understood how it works. We know that there are three stages, and we know there are parts of the brain where memory seems to be centralized. We even know that the human memory has an enormous capacity, if you can stimulate it and store information in an optimal manner.

However, we don't understand why there are such big differences in memory performance between different people, and we certainly don't understand cases of exceptional memory, such as displayed by savants or hyperthymesiacs.

In this chapter, I want to talk about phenomena of memory—rare instances in which our memory can act in ways that shock and surprise us with no clear explanation. Our memory can truly be the stuff that movies are based on, so let's start with the phenomena that you've probably seen movies about: amnesia.

Amnesia

Amnesia, as you may be aware, is the loss of memory. There are two types of amnesia: anterograde and retrograde.

Retrograde amnesia is when you are incapable of recalling information before a certain event or date. If Bob has retrograde amnesia, he cannot remember anything from *before* he hit his head. However, Bob can form new memories, and even study for school effectively after hitting his head. This is the type of amnesia that is more frequently depicted in movies because it easily creates a sense of intrigue about a character. Bob likely knows his name, who he is married to, and what he does, but he does not know specific details.

Anterograde amnesia is when you are incapable of storing new information as a long-term memory after a certain event or date. If Bob has anterograde amnesia, he cannot remember anything from *after* he hit his head. Bob, however, can remember long-term memories from before he hit his head. In a sense, Bob will be living in the past forever, as each day will feel like the same day from a lack of long-term memories.

Unfortunately, both types of amnesia may occur in the same person at the same time. The type of amnesia one is afflicted with typically depends on the area of the brain that is damaged.

There are three general methods through which one can get amnesia:

- Traumatic injury
- Traumatic events
- Physical atrophy

Phenomena of Memory

Traumatic injury is an obvious cause. If you are struck in the head without a helmet on, you can cause serious brain injury and swelling in the cranium. This can be an accident, as most instances are, or it can be intentional, such as undergoing the infamous surgical procedure of a lobotomy.

Traumatic events are entirely mental and depend on the person's state of mind. A traumatic event is where someone experiences something that is so stressful and alarming for them, their mind acts to defend itself and repress the memories. You might hear of this when people talk about childhood abuse or domestic violence. The memories have been processed, but they have been shut out of the person's consciousness for the time being. This, of course, is related to dissociative identity disorder, which is more commonly known as multiple personality disorder.

Physical atrophy is different from a traumatic injury in that someone's brain might begin to degenerate due to drug use, age, or surgery that changes the structure of the brain. All three of these causes can damage the areas where memory is stored, processed, or encoded. As you've read, there are numerous processes involved in creating a memory, from the movement of the eye, an understanding that you are seeing a bird, moving the bird from sensory memory to short-term memory, then rehearsing and encoding the bird into long-term memory. There are countless points where the memory process can break down due to the underlying hardware or software failing.

Amnesia is not entirely understood, except as a series of injuries or failings of the memory system to encode, store, or retrieve memories. Perhaps one of the best illustrations of how amnesia can truly affect someone is the curious case of Clive Wearing, who was diagnosed with powerful anterograde memory loss in 1985. It wasn't just a normal case of amnesia (both anterograde and retrograde)—he only had a memory span of somewhere from seven to 30 seconds.

In other words, on average, he would completely forget where he was, what he was doing, and who he was with every 18 seconds. He might not even remember people if he had just met them and was conversing with them, tending to trail off in mid-sentence. Every day was a process of coming back into consciousness after an average of 18 seconds. The last thing he remembered was a point before his diagnosis, and then he'd come back into his own version of consciousness, standing and speaking with strangers. It was like he was blacking out constantly, then awaking and thinking it was some point in 1985—every 18 seconds.

Suppose people blink an average of five times in 18 seconds. This means every five times Wearing blinked, it was as if his eyes opened to a new view.

Wearing was an accomplished musician with BBC Radio, so you can imagine how his inability to store new memories affected him. He couldn't learn any new music, and looking at any piece of music he hadn't seen before his diagnosis turned it into an entirely new piece of music that had to be re-learned. He would never be able to learn a new instrument, and he would never be able to improve his skills as a musician, singer, conductor, or composer. Professionally, he was stuck in one place. He could still play piano, but that was from a combination of muscle memory and procedural memory, which was not touched by his amnesia.

Personally, it was much worse. He knew he had children, but couldn't remember their names. He knew he loved his wife, but he occasionally believed they had never met, even though they married in 1985. He was sometimes unable to link food with its taste because he forgot what he was eating by the time he tasted it.

A closer look inside Wearing's thought processes can be gleaned from reading his diary. He wanted to record "waking up for the first time," and he still wrote diary entries recording this event in 2007, over two decades after he started them. He didn't know how the entries were made, but he did recognize his own handwriting.

Wearing lives in a world where he lives and dies in the span of 18 seconds, and repeats it every day.

Flashbulb Memories

A flashbulb memory is a memory that feels like you can reach out and touch it still. It is incredibly vivid, clear, and detailed. For example, do you remember where you were and what you were doing the moment you heard or read about the tragedy of 9/11?

I remember watching the attack on the World Trade Center on television at school, and hearing the school announcements while in a daze in my biology class. The voice on the intercom was close to tears, and the rest of the people in the classroom were sitting in stunned silence. The professor wasn't present at the time, but I remember the person sitting next to me gasping and grabbing her blue sweater tightly. I was wearing black Nike shoes, and halfway through, the professor walked into the classroom.

You likely have a very strong emotional pull to that memory, and you remember everything about that exact moment. Older people might have flashbulb memories of the assassinations of prominent national figures or when family members died, or even the time they witnessed a car accident. This is the essence of flashbulb memories: they are tied to significant and emotional events, either personal or historical.

Something about the emotional fixation and arousal of the moment helps cement that particular moment in time as a powerful memory that is often remembered until death. Because of the emotional impact, flashbulb memories are typically assumed to involve the amygdala, one of the brain's main processing centers for emotion.

The term "flashbulb memories" was coined in 1977 by Brown and Kulik, who proposed that they existed and were forever etched into our brains as an evolutionary defense mechanism. Suppose you were attacked by a wild animal, something which would cause a flashbulb memory because it is so emotionally traumatic and impactful. Brown and Kulik hypothesized the use of flashbulb memories was so we can go back in time, at the moment of danger, and analyze in great detail how we can avoid similar situations in the future.

Phenomena of Memory

Strong emotional impact is the genesis of a flashbulb memory. Therefore, whether flashbulb memories are formed is largely subjective. You might have a slightly fuzzy memory of your flashbulb memory of 9/11—but I would ask that you try to recall what you did later that day, September 10th, and September 12th. I would be willing to bet that those details are all lost forever, not even bothered to be committed to long-term memory at all. Flashbulb memories live in our minds with vivid detail for decades after they occur, as if we had rehearsed them ad nauseam and attempted to commit them to memory intentionally.

Flashbulb memories are intense, but they have been shown to be less than reliable. As you've read in this book, our memories are highly susceptible to manipulation, whether they get mixed up with fantasy or daydream, they degrade naturally, are skewed by our natural biases, or they are influenced by other accounts.

For example, if you develop a flashbulb memory around 9/11, your account could shift according to:

- How you daydreamed about making an impromptu patriotic speech in front of your family.
- What your friends told you about 9/11 and their flashbulb memories surrounding it.
- How you feel about 9/11 and your reaction.

Why is this important to note?

It just emphasizes the fact that memory is highly suggestible, which is the last phenomena of memory I want to cover in this chapter. If something we feel lives in a snapshot in our brains can be found to be falsified and wrong, something we are so confident and sure about, then what does that mean for our other memories? Memories that are unremarkable and common—what's to stop them from being easily confused, mixed up, or entirely planted and fabricated?

Unfortunately, nothing.

False Memories

More frequently than we would like to admit, we have false memories, we remember incorrectly, or we are flat-out wrong about what happened in the past.

Just because our memories are capable of remarkable feats doesn't mean that they aren't subject to errors that are just as remarkable. A false memory is simply a memory that is real, which is neurologically identical to a real memory, but not based on something that actually happened.

In 1995, Loftus and Coan from the University of California, Irvine conducted a simple study to investigate how to implant a false memory by fusing it with an existing, real memory. The study involved a subject who was given descriptions of three true memories from his childhood, and one false memory. The subject wrote about each of the four memories for five days in a row, giving a summary and any details or facts he could remember about each of the memories (three real and one false).

Over the five days, the subject began to recall more and more about the false memory, introducing details that were never there, and that seemed to stem completely from the subject's imagination. He purported to remember everyone that was present, and even the emotions involved. He was adding onto the false memory, not realizing it was made up.

Weeks later, the subject was asked to rate his memories for how clear they were. He gave the false memory the second highest rating out of the four memories presented. He could provide vivid detail—perhaps because it was fabricated, so the details conformed to his idea of what the idea would usually entail. Memories could be implanted in people just by saying that they had occurred.

Memories, if they are not entirely false or fabricated, can also be influenced by things as small as suggestive word choice, phrasing, and vocabulary. An infamous study conducted in 1974 by Loftus and Palmer at the University of California, Irvine illustrates this effect.

Subjects watched different videos of car accidents at three different speeds. After, they filled out a survey which asked, "About how fast were the cars going when they *smashed* into each other?"

Other groups of subjects watched the exact same videos and filled out a survey after as well, but the survey instead asked, "About how fast were the cars going when they *bumped/hit/contacted* each other?" The estimates the subjects gave changed in relation to the verb used, which influenced the perception of speed and impact.

- Smashed = 40.8 mph
- Bumped = 38.1 mph

- Hit = 34 mph
- Contacted = 31.8 mph

This simple change in vocabulary affected people's perception of an event, and in essence changed their memory surrounding it. How reliable can memory truly be when we are manipulated by such small things? This was an event that the subjects watched on video—and the speed increased by nearly 10 mph when leading language was used—a discrepancy of 25%.

The ease with which false memories are created are why eyewitness testimony occupies such an ambivalent place in the legal system. Memories can change during interrogation, and sometimes intentionally. For example, Annalies Vredeveldt of the University of Amsterdam states that asking questions about a memory can easily take a wrong turn, if for example, you ask questions as simple as, "What was the color of his hair?" or "He was a redhead, wasn't he?" The first question assumes that there was a male, and the second question is leading and draws its own conclusions.

Eyewitness accounts are highly trusted by juries, yet highly condemned by judges and attorneys who know better. Researcher Julia Shaw states that to implant a false memory, "you try to get someone to confuse their imagination with their memory and get them to repeatedly picture it happening."

This means simply repeating a false memory or story to someone can cause them to confuse the false memory with reality, and eventually mesh together with the real account. There is a very thin and blurry line between memory and imagination.

Eyewitness testimony has been questioned since Hugo Munsterberg's seminal 1908 book *On the Witness Stand*. He questioned the reliability of memory and perception, and the legal community has taken notice ever since. What's scary is that research has shown that juries can't tell the difference between false and accurate witness testimony, often simply relying on how confident the eyewitness is (Nicholson, 2014). As we learned in the section about flashbulb memories, confidence is never the hallmark of accuracy. Additional support for the distrust in eyewitness testimony has been found in analyses by Scheck and Neufel, who showed that eyewitness testimony was frequently present in cases that were later exonerated based on DNA evidence.

With the knowledge of how unreliable memory can be and just how easy it is to implant false or biased memories, it's a wonder eyewitness testimony is still allowed.

Christopher French of the University of London sums it up best: *"There is currently no way to distinguish, in the absence of independent evidence, whether a particular memory is true or false. Even memories which are detailed and vivid and held with 100 percent conviction can be completely false."*

Our memories are incredible, but the same malleability that leads to memory feats can also be exploited to show great flaws.

10

BOOST YOUR BRAIN

A healthy brain doesn't just improve your memory—it also improves your brain power. In this final chapter, I want to present a few science-based pieces of advice on how to get your brain functioning at its best for when you need it the most. You might recognize or instinctually know some of these tips, but that doesn't mean you understand *why* they matter. You could be engaging in something beneficial, but for the wrong reason, and thus not understand how to optimize your results.

For example, it does seem intuitive that having relationships and friendships can help your brain's functioning, but how exactly does it work? Is there a better way of interacting with people on a regular basis that helps your brain keep fit? This is the first piece of improving your overall brain health that I'll tackle and explain.

Social Interaction

Studies led by researchers at the University of Michigan have highlighted just how important getting consistent and regular social interaction is to the brain's cognitive abilities.

They had three groups of subjects that took a brain performance test. The first group did nothing before the test, the second group was paired up with random people and instructed to interact with them for 10 minutes, and the third group received brain game activities for 10 minutes.

What resulted were two tiers: In the bottom tier was the first group, who routinely performed the worst, while the second and third groups were on the upper tier and performed better on the test. Brain performance was activated and primed to the same degree just from simply talking to someone and asking them questions as it was for brain games designed for that very purpose. What conclusions could the researchers theoretically draw from the results?

Primarily, conversation stimulates our brains a heck of a lot more than we realize. Conversation in and of itself is a complex process that requires encoding of what we hear and see, analysis on a level of micro-seconds, and composing an appropriate and related response. Sometimes conversation forces us to draw on our long-term and short-term memories and activates our hippocampus and prefrontal cortex, and other times it is purely emotional and activates our amygdala.

Conversation is like a Choose-Your-Own-Adventure book—it can go just about anywhere, and as such, activates a variety of brain regions depending on the topic and context. Thus, it makes sense that if you were to stick to a script that talks through a range of topics and emotions, your brain would be "warmed up" for performance. In fact, you might be better warmed up than if you participated in a brain-game, because a brain game is going to be logical and mentally strenuous—but it won't activate various parts of the brain.

Social interaction as a whole is unpredictable, and keeps us on our toes—that is, if we are engaged. It's no different than solving a riddle or a puzzle.

In 2008, Professor Oscar Ybarra of the University of Michigan investigated whether social interaction merely warmed our brains up for performance like jumping jacks for hamstrings, or actually improved our mental faculties. In other words, could social interaction be a key to better cognition, memory, and thinking?

Ybarra found that people who engaged in greater amounts of social interaction indeed displayed higher levels of cognitive test performance—there was a strong correlation between social interaction and better thinking, essentially. Of course, correlation does not equal causation, so it cannot be said that social interaction specifically causes better thinking—it can only be said that people who engage more socially perform better cognitively. You can't tell which is influencing which, if there even is a causal relationship of any type.

This can mean that people who are smarter tend to engage more socially, or even that there is a third factor responsible for both these effects. We can easily imagine the well-rounded person who is both smart and social, but we can also imagine the shy introvert who expresses themselves best through their work. It's hard to say, but given that there is a strong correlation between cognitive ability and social interaction, it's something we can practice every day to think a bit more quickly on our feet.

Studies have been conducted amongst the elderly to investigate the relationship between social interaction and memory, and they have found similar benefits (Ertel, 2008). However, they have been able to answer the question because they were able to study these subjects over longer periods of time, including before their memories started to decline. They found the elderly who reported high amounts of social interaction *before* memory decline were the ones that still engaged in it *after* memory decline.

It has also been theorized that having better relationships and being in contact with a social support is a source of comfort, and consequently, less stress—recall the vastly damaging effects stress can have on your memory capacity.

Neural Adaptation

Neural adaptation is the brain's ability to change and adapt according to new stimuli, experience, or information. When you remove all of those factors, your brain removes any reason to keep growing and changing.

Essentially, it's good practice to keep the brain challenged and stimulated, as opposed to stagnant and bored. When you give your brain constant challenges and stimulation, it will stay sharp and continue its neural adaptation. If you let your brain fall into routines and fail to exercise it, it will begin to degrade, especially as you grow older.

Human brains are changed on a daily basis by a concept called neural plasticity, which is the idea that the brain is malleable. It can change, wrinkle, grow, and shrink depending on what it experiences. Of course, we want our brains to have neural plasticity of the positive kind—where the brain is expanding, learning, and digesting new information.

For example, learning a new language, or even a skill like playing an instrument, can cause massive physical changes in the brain related to the neurons, synapses, and memory structures in the hippocampus. These keep us mentally fit and alert because we are stimulating the parts of our brain that aid us in everyday life.

Taxi drivers have been shown to have larger hippocampus than average because the hippocampus deals with spatial information that taxi drivers use in creating routes, seeing directions, and analyzing maps (Maguire, 2006). Bilingual people also have differentiated brain structure as compared to monolingual people (Mechelli, 2004). Clearly, there is a biological basis for keeping our brains in shape.

So, how can you generate neural adaptation in your everyday life?

Learn consistently. You can read, watch videos, or look at infographics, if you want—the point is that the act of learning new information, making sense of it, processing it, attaching emotional significance to it, and then committing some of it to long-term memory will exercise your brain and stimulate it to a high degree. If you don't want to learn a new skill or take up a new hobby, per se, just consume more information. Commit at least 10 minutes of your day to reading something unfamiliar and broaden your horizons. Not only is this good for your social skills and sense of the world, it will stimulate your brain and push your boundaries. This includes new hobbies, sports, instruments, and activities that require you to learn new information, movements, or anything you aren't familiar with already.

Author James Altucher champions writing 10 new ideas each day. The ideas don't have to be good, they don't have to be related, and they don't even have to make sense. What's important is that you simply start writing out ideas every day. You will find that it's a muscle that you can cultivate and exercise. Specifically, it is the muscle of creativity, innovation, and abstract thinking.

You don't have to do anything with your ideas, and they don't have to serve any purpose. You can throw them away, and you don't have to see them ever again. Make your metric of success the act of generating the ideas, not how *good* they are. If the ideas are good, they'll probably inspire you to action or further thought, anyway. Pick a simple category and write 10 ideas for it, or just write 10 abstract ideas or thoughts that spring into your mind when you are staring at a blank piece of paper (a category on its own, admittedly).

Follow Your Rhythm

Your circadian rhythm, to be specific. Your circadian rhythm is the biological cycle that dictates how you adapt to a 24-hour day. It controls when you feel sleepy, when you want to wake up, and when you are at your highest peaks of energy and alertness. There is a particular ebb and flow each day because it's impossible to stay on high alert 24 hours a day, so the body has learned to pick and choose when throughout the years. You don't get sleepy after lunch because you are digesting; you get sleepy because of your circadian rhythm.

Your circadian rhythm is what jet lag affects, and why you can't simply go to bed extremely early and instantly fall asleep if you want to catch up on your sleep. Why does this matter for better thinking? Think of it this way: You are going to be a much more effective thinker if you can do your toughest work when you are at your best.

Studies have shown that people tend to peak in mental alertness and alacrity at roughly noon, and then 6 PM each day, ebbing and flowing between each peak, and finally reaching its nadir at roughly 3:30 AM (Taylor & Francis, 2000). Thus, it makes sense to do your tasks that require the greatest amount of creativity, ingenuity, and thought around your daily peaks, and then save your easy tasks for any other time. Take advantage of when your brain is naturally at its best.

However, if you're saying to yourself that you're more of a morning bird or night owl, that might be true, and it is generally a genetic difference between some people (Ptacek, University of

California). However, the overall curve of the circadian rhythm remains unchanged in people; whether you are a "lark" or an "owl", you still have similar peaks and valleys of mental alertness. This type of circadian programming also applies to your physical peaks, which happen to coincide roughly with your mental peaks at 3 PM to 6 PM (Smolensky, University of Texas, Austin).

Perhaps even Einstein did his best thinking before lunch and before dinner.

Feed Your Body Right

What your mother told you actually has roots in truth. There are foods that you could classify as good for your brain, but they might not be peas, carrots, and vegetables. Feeding your body so it performs to its peak abilities is about giving your brain the nutrients it wants and needs.

Omega-3 fatty acids aren't produced in the body, which means you must consume them. They've been shown to help brain function and are biologically beneficial to the neurons that make up our brain cells. Sixty percent of the human brain is fat (Chang CY, 2009), so omega-3 fatty acids can be said to contribute heavily to the structural integrity of the brain. Glucose, what most food is converted to inside the body, is also the brain's primary source of power.

Finally, omega-3 fatty acids contain EPA and DHA, which act as anti-inflammatories. The main sources of this healthy type of fat are either through supplements, or oily fish such as salmon, sardines, or trout.

Perhaps more fundamental and important than omega-3 fatty acids is simply staying as hydrated as possible. If you aren't hydrated, studies have shown reaction times to decrease by up to 14% (University of East London, 2013). When you're thirsty, your brain is literally busy with the thought of water and how to stave off starvation. In other words, a dehydrated brain is using up to 14% of its resources dealing with feeling thirsty, and you can free up those valuable resources simply by staying hydrated.

Water provides the brain with electrical energy for all of its functions, such as thought and memory formation. Brain cells require twice as much energy as other cells in the body, so it makes sense that dehydration would affect your thinking efficacy. After all, your brain can't store it, so it needs a constant supply ready for use, and ready to fuel your focus and clarity of thought.

Studies have shown that if you are only 1% dehydrated, you are likely to have up to a 5% decrease in cognitive function. That rate of decrease compounds the more you get dehydrated. If your memory starts getting fuzzy and you have trouble focusing at 2% dehydration, imagine the complications you'll have at 5-10% dehydration. Further studies have shown that prolonged dehydration causes brain cells to shrink in size and mass. This is most common in the elderly, many of whom tend to be chronically dehydrated for years. Water is also essential for delivering nutrients to the brain and for removing toxins. When the brain is fully hydrated, the exchange of nutrients and toxins will be more efficient—thus ensuring better concentration and mental alertness.

In short, make a habit of carrying a water bottle around with you. You don't need to drink 64 ounces of water daily, as some people might suggest, but you could almost certainly stand to benefit from drinking more than you currently do.

The final overarching tip in eating healthy is to eat to reduce inflammation in your brain. I mentioned this earlier, but inflammation in your brain occurs when special brain cells called microglia are activated (Elmore, 2014). Inflammation in the brain causes neurons to fire more slowly, delaying mental acuity, recall, and reflexes. Sluggish neurons also shut down the production of energy in the cells. This means that cells fatigue easily, and you may lose your ability to focus for long periods of time.

Unfortunately, there are a whole host of things that tend to activate the microglia, some of the primary ones being sugar, dairy, and gluten. However, there are foods that are naturally anti-inflammatory, such as ginger, green vegetables, and turmeric.

CONCLUSION

To this day, I tell the story of remembering state capitals to friends of mine who turned out to be teachers, and they marvel at its simplicity. It's no easy feat to calm a 10-year-old down and subject him to 50 separate pieces of information, but to do it effortlessly and without them knowing is something special.

Improving your memory, as you can see, doesn't require a tremendous brain with special capabilities. Even memory champions who can memorize and recite pi to thousands of decimals, or who can memorize decks of cards in 30 seconds—they have all self-reported as having average memories, and indeed, this has been confirmed by memory tests.

One of the most prominent memory competitors in recent history, Joshua Foer, author of the bestseller *Moonwalking with Einstein*, only began his memory studies as a journalism experiment. One year later, he was competing for a national championship.

Your memory capacity is far greater than you think. You already use memory devices and you don't even know it. Whenever I go somewhere and need to remember a few

Conclusion

pieces of information, I feed them into the combination of my overactive imagination + memory palace and am on my way.

You don't have to compete for a memory championship to greatly improve your memory skills. Memory enables just about everything we want to achieve, so there's no better time to start than now!

Best,
Pete

SUMMARY GUIDE

Chapter 1. How Memory Works

Memory is a three-part process: encoding, storage, and retrieval. There are many aspects within each part of the process, but all of memory, from the feats to the flaws, can usually be explained by one of those three parts.

Chapter 2. All About Forgetting

Forgetting is usually an error in one of the three parts of memory, not simply a memory that fades away due to time. We forget at a specific rate according to Ebbinghaus' Forgetting Curve.

Chapter 3. The Roles of Stress, Sleep, and Exercise

Stress puts you in a chronic state of arousal and anxiety, which makes you physiologically unable to focus or relax. Sleep recharges our brains for optimal performance, and exercise creates BDNF and other hormones which are beneficial for better brain function.

Chapter 4. Memory Improvement Methods Pt. I

This first chapter on memory improvement methods contains: spaced repetition, mnemonics, creating stories or narratives, and the peg word method.

Chapter 5. Memory Improvement Methods Pt. II

This second chapter on memory improvement methods contains: teaching for better synthesis, utilizing more of your senses and sensory memory, the Zeigarnik Effect, and the Recency Effect and Primacy Effect.

Chapter 6. Memory Improvement Methods Pt. III

This third chapter on memory improvement methods contains: the Von Restorff Effect and our preference for visual imagery, drawing, chunking, meditation, and the Major System.

Chapter 7. The Memory Palace Technique

The memory palace, also known as the method of loci technique, involves visualizing walking through a location you are familiar with, and combining new information with the visual route you are walking.

Chapter 8. Developing Photographic Memory

Photographic memory as depicted in movies has not been proven to exist, but eidetic memory can be trained to some degree by what is known as the military method.

Chapter 9. Phenomena of Memory

The brain can behave in fabulously exceptional and unusual ways. There are two main types of amnesia, flashbulb memories imprint on your mind, and a proliferation of false memories can be easily implanted or fabricated.

Chapter 10. Boost Your Brain

Boosting your brain benefits your memory capabilities. You can do this by socializing more, challenging yourself with neural adaptation, finding your optimal circadian rhythm, and feeding your body (and brain) exactly what it needs.